THE EROTIC IMAGINATION

SEXUAL FANTASIES OF THE ADULT MALE

WILLIAM J. SLATTERY

HENRY REGNERY COMPANY • CHICAGO

Library of Congress Cataloging in Publication Data

Slattery, William James, 1930-
  The erotic imagination.

  1. Sex (Psychology)   2. Fantasy.   I. Title.
BF692.55   154.3   74-6909
ISBN 0-8092-8368-9

Copyright © 1975 By William J. Slattery

Copyright © by William J. Slattery
All rights reserved
Published by Henry Regnery Company
180 North Michigan Avenue, Chicago, Illinois 60601
Manufactured in the United States of America
Library of Congress Catalog Card Number: 74-6909
International Standard Book Number: 0-8092-8368-9

Published simultaneously in Canada by
Fitzhenry & Whiteside Limited
150 Lesmill Road
Don Mills, Ontario M3B 2T5
Canada

CONTENTS

Foreword by Robert Chartham, Ph.D. v

Introduction viii

1 Heterosexual Fantasies 1

2 Homosexual Fantasies 81

3 Bisexual Fantasies 99

4 Sadomasochistic Fantasies 121

5 Assorted Fetishes 145

   Afterword 177

FOREWORD

Most of us have a Walter Mitty element in our makeup. No matter what our real-life circumstances are and no matter how happy those circumstances make us, we all have secret yearnings for something different—the millionaire to be a poor man, the garbage collector to be an oil sheik, the tone-deaf man to be a musical virtuoso. These secret yearnings we translate into daydreams, and I believe that if we made a tally of the time we spend daydreaming, we would be surprised at the number of hours in the year that we devote to this activity.

It might be suggested that daydreaming (or fantasizing) is a waste of time that might be more gainfully employed. No so. For most people, fantasizing is a safety valve through which we give vent to the frustrations that our unfulfilled secret longings might create. If our imaginations are fairly vivid, while we are actually fantasizing we can make our fantasy-world seem so real that our secret desires are as satisfied as they would be were our fantasies to become fact.

If this is true of the nonsexual areas of our lives, it is even more true of our sexual experience. More and more people are learning to shed their sexual inhibitions, but there are still vast numbers who just haven't the courage to behave with the complete sexual abandon that can provide the ultimate measure of physical and emotional satisfaction we would all like to achieve from the expression of our sexuality. The ethical and religious restraints under which we have been molding our sex lives, for the last 150 years at least, are even today having a tremendous influence on our sexual behavior; and the feelings of guilt, sin, and shame that any so-called unorthodox sexual activity or desire generate, are sufficiently powerful to prevent us from setting ourselves sexually free. In consequence, possibly the only way in which we can limit, though not entirely eliminate, the frustrations that our unfulfilled secret sexual longings create, is by fantasizing.

As I have been shouting from the house-tops for more than a decade—though still with only a very partial success—we are all entitled to the sexual experience, and it doesn't matter how we achieve it provided neither partner is physically or emotionally hurt. I would far rather that this were applied to the way in which we physically respond to our sexual urges; but if anyone is inhibited from doing so, then fantasizing is fully justified as an alternative.

And yet, while it is true that many men and women are able to fantasize without compunction, many still have guilt feelings about doing so. That this is true, is very evident from the contents of this book.

I still have men and women writing to me, saying, "My husband keeps asking me to suck his penis. But surely this isn't natural? I love him very much and would like to do it for him, but if I did would I not be as kinky as he is?" Or, "My husband wants to enter me from the rear, what I believe is called 'doggie fashion.' Wouldn't I be degrading myself if I let him use me like an animal, though I must admit it would be an exciting change from always doing it with one or other of us on top?" Or, "My wife keeps asking me to rub her nipple with my penis and shoot all my semen all over her breast. I have done it once or twice, and it does excite her very much. She comes much more quickly when I do it, than when we fuck in the ordinary way. But I don't know whether I should go on doing it, because it isn't normal, is it?" Or, "My girl friend likes to watch me whacking off while she rubs herself off. I have to admit I find it quite exciting, but doesn't it make us both kinky?"

If people are worried about innocuous activities such as these—all of which are perfectly valid sexual activities—many are even more worried about their fantasy activities. Just as the "doers" seek for reassurance, so the fantasizer needs reassurance. But unless he goes to a psychiatrist, psychologist, or counselor, he won't hear what he wants to hear; and, in any case, to consult an expert usually seems so drastic—besides, it would mean revealing one's most secret sexual thoughts face to face, an act requiring more courage than is generally appreciated.

Herein, I believe, lies the intrinsic value of this book.

I have been counselling now for over forty years. From time to time I say to myself, "I've heard it all!" and the very next second I hear something I have *not* heard before. Many of the fantasies in this book can only be described as bizarre. If anyone with what might be termed an "ordinary" fantasy about which he is worried reads these more way-out fantasies, he can not fail to be reassured. Similarly, for those who have described their more extreme fantasies, there will be reassurance in the knowledge that many others have the same vivid sexual imagination.

Not least, however, this collection of fantasies will be of value to the various categories of experts in the sexual counselling field; for fantasies not only reveal the secret longings of the fantasizer, but also his sexual characteristics. For example, it is possible to tell from an analysis of a fantasy that a man has feelings of sexual inadequacy, or that he desires to be dominant at all costs, or to be dominated, or that he has latent homosexual desires, or that he has suppressed masochistic or sadistic tendencies, and so on.

It would be possible to talk with such a man (or woman) for several hours and not learn as much as one would from a twenty-minute recital of a fantasy or fantasies. Unfortunately, I only realized this three or four years ago, but now, when a man or woman, comes to me, after listening to a brief outline of the basic problem, I ask them to describe their fantasies. Some will deny fantasizing at all, but with a little coaxing, most of them will come across. The time saved is considerable; and time in my sort of work, is valuable.

My good friend Bill Slattery has performed a great service in collecting these fantasies, both for the fantasizers and for people like myself. He has produced a book that I urge should be widely read for the comfort it will afford to many, and for the extended knowledge it imparts to those qualified to use such material.

Robert Chartham, Ph.D.

INTRODUCTION

The fantasies collected here have been gathered over a five-year period. They are the fantasies of as broad a cross section of men as one researcher working less than full time could possibly gather. Among people talked to in the course of preparing the book were barbers and bartenders, writers, editors, actors, musicians, photographers, directors, plumbers, politicians, gangsters, airline pilots, cab drivers, doctors, farmers, military men, sexologists, delivery boys, barflies, junkies, one jewel thief, and one Mafia hit man.

Some of the sexual fantasies are pure fantasies and involve situations and events that are entirely fanciful. "Beneath the surface of the earth is a vast continent populated entirely by women. I am the emperor of this world. My only imperial duty is to fuck every one of my subjects every day. I am a very good emperor. My subjects all love me." This kind of fantasy is rare. The man who had this particular one is a convicted rapist.

Most fantasies are about events men wish would happen to them. "My girlfriend called me on the telephone last Sunday and asked me over to her place. When I arrived she greeted me naked at the door. She told me to take my clothes off. While I was undressing she went into the bedroom. I could hear other voices. I went into the bedroom. There were two other girls there all licking and sucking away at each other. I sat on the foot of the bed and began stroking myself. After a while I got a giant hard on. The four of us stayed in bed all day Sunday, all Sunday night, and all the next day and the next night. I have no idea how many orgasms I had. Maybe fifty, maybe a hundred. I never lost the erection and my cock never got sore. It was a glorious experience."

This particular fantasy was told to me by an actor, a man in his forties. He is happily and faithfully married and does not have a girlfriend. He has never been to an orgy in his life. He reports that he has been invited to a number of orgies but that he does not have the guts to go. He would like to go but he can't stand the thought of someone else fucking his wife.

This fantasy stimulates both the actor and his wife. He has been telling this little tale to her, with thousands of variations, for nearly twenty years, a sort of bedtime story. It turns them both on, and they say they have a great sex life. In the hundreds and hundreds of interviews I have conducted, this is the commonest type of fantasy. The man uses the fantasy to arouse himself prior to masturbation or intercourse with a partner or partners. The content of the fantasy is something that could actually happen, something the man wishes would actually happen but hasn't the nerve to carry through.

Another common fantasy is recollective. The man remembers some past sexual experience that was particularly pleasurable. He runs it through his mind for the rest of his life because recalling the event gives him great sexual pleasure. Recollections qualify as fantasies because the actual event is heavily edited and what is remembered is not the actual event but just the best parts of what actually happened.

Roughly half the fantasies in this book are recollective. Most of the remainder are projections of what men wish they had the courage to do. Those few fantasies that lie outside these categories seem, at times, dark and horrible. Hopefully, they are just fantasies, and are not acted out in real life.

In the last year of my research, it suddenly occurred to me that all the fantasies I was collecting came from normal men. They were people I met in the course of my work, at parties, my friends, their friends, people I sat next to on planes and trains and in bars. I was, I realized, neglecting abnormal men. A number of psychiatrists, psychiatric social workers, psychologists, sex counselors, and marriage counselors were helpful in discussing the fantasies of their patients. But helpful as these professionals were, it soon became apparent that the information I was getting from them lacked any feel for reality. The fantasies they provided were often detailed and bizarre. But they were also clinical and detached and somehow a little dull. I decided to talk directly with men who could easily have been their patients.

Under a false name I placed a small advertisement in the personal columns of a number of publications, both national and local. The ad said that I was collecting men's sexual fantasies and requested people to call in their fantasies to me or to write them and send them to a post office box.

The ads were overwhelmingly effective. For a start, I received some five hundred telephone calls. Many, but by no means all, of these people were freaks of one kind or another. They called to ask if they could fuck my wife, me, my children, my dogs and cats, and the furniture. One guy wanted to come over and masturbate into my refrigerator. Dozens called to ask if I would piss, shit, or masturbate on them, in them, around them or their wives, lovers, children, and animals. Dozens more wanted to come over and have me beat them with whips, chairs, razor straps, belts, shoes, and underwear. Scores wanted to dress me in women's clothes and fuck me. Dozens just called to chat while they masturbated.

And in addition to the freaks, I got calls and letters from dozens of seriously disturbed men. Rapists, child molesters, obscene telephone callers, the heavy breathers, necrophiliacs, genital mutilators, professional masters and slaves, coprophiliacs, men who pleaded with me to let them speak to my wife so they could shout obscenities at her, men who wanted to hear me rub the telephone against my genitals while they did the same thing.

A large percentage of people who called in response to my advertisements hung up the minute I answered the phone. Many others said something like, "Oh, hell, I thought I had the nerve to tell you, but I don't. I'll call later." They seldom did. And there were those who whispered or mumbled a few words and hung up. Following are some of the whispers and mumbles:

* * * * I drill holes in her nipples and put a chain through and lead her around the house like a dog. * * * *

* * * * I'm a married fag with children. I think I will kill myself. * * * *

* * * * If I knew your address, I'd go there and kill you. It's God's will. You are filth. * * * *

Introduction xi

* * * * I've invented the Russian kiss. I come in her mouth. She kisses me and puts the come in my mouth. I go down on her and blow it into her cunt. * * * *

* * * * I pour ice water in her. I put a balloon in her and blow it up. * * * *

* * * * I have a brass four-poster. She rides up and down on a post. * * * *

* * * * I shove beer bottles in both places, and she puts one in me. * * * *

* * * * I smear her ass with peanut butter. Jesus. * * * *

* * * * She likes me to shove this long rubber thing in her, put a rubber raincoat on her, handcuffs, and make her walk the streets at night. The rubber thing bulges out and people can see it. We both like this. * * * *

* * * * Is there a woman or a child with you now? I want to talk to one of them and touch myself. Well, fuck you. * * * *

* * * * They're all whores, every goddamned one of them, even my mother and yours and my wife and daughters and the Virgin Mary. Did you know that Christ had brothers? Can you imagine the mother of God giving her husband a blow job? My confessor says I should see a psychiatrist. He tells me that Christ wasn't fucking those whores. The Bible doesn't say he wasn't. Guys who hang out with whores are either pimps or johns, right? So what does that make him, right? * * * *

As alarming as some of the calls were, many of the fantasies tended to be more interesting than those of my acquaintances because the men were out of control and without inhibition. But, although their fantasies were somewhat more detailed than other men's, they do not differ in kind. I have discussed this curious fact with a number of psychiatrists, who say that the sexual fantasies of "normal" and "abnormal" men are identical. Or, in other words, there is no such thing as an abnormal fantasy.

Fantasy, according to the psychiatrists, serves two functions. It gives pleasure to the individual and stability to society. Many men fantasize dangerous and cruel little dramas inside their heads, which, if acted out in the real world, would cause pain and trauma to others and land the fantasizer in jail. But they do not act out the fantasies. The fantasies give such men release. By having the fantasies, they dispel their antisocial tendencies and behave as normal men. In fact, they *are* normal men because "normal" is a behavioral word. A man is normal if he acts normally.

Many of the fantasies in this collection were told to me by men in the public eye—actors, politicians, athletes, writers, and other famous folk. I have guaranteed these men complete anonymity in exchange for their fantasies. In fact, everyone is well disguised—even the author.

You will note as your read that all the fantasies reported here seem to come from reasonably literate, educated men. This is not at all the case, as mentioned a moment ago. What you will be reading has been heavily edited and rewritten and reorganized to make the fantasies as brief as possible and interesting to read. However, in no case have I tampered with the facts presented by whomever I was interviewing.

I am sure you will find much in what follows that repels you. There is certainly much in what follows that repels me. Many times during the writing of the book I set it aside and worked on other projects until I could once again face the terrible jottings in my notebooks, the ugly words on the tapes. I gather from psychiatrist friends who have read the manuscript that the material contained herein is reasonably routine stuff they hear every day from their patients in the course of their work. I certainly do not find the contents of the book routine. If you are a layman and not a psychiatrist, I trust you, like me, will find many surprises, not all of them uplifting.

Although any attempt to classify the fantasies contained in this book will be, of necessity, somewhat arbitrary, some general scheme of classification is needed just to handle the volume of letters and telephone calls I received. I have chosen the most obvious method of classification open to me, that of the sexual orientation upon which the fantasies are based. Thus, fantasies that are basically heterosexual in content, with the exception of sadomasochistic and fetishistic fantasies, are all grouped together in Chapter 1. I have intentionally kept my comments to a minimum, preferring to leave matters of judgment to the reader.

1

HETEROSEXUAL FANTASIES

DRIVING HOME

* * * * I love my wife, even though she's just about the dullest lady I have ever been to bed with. She gives me all the sex I want, which is fine and the way it should be. But she has zero imagination and no willingness to experiment. When we make love, she lies on her back and spreads her legs and takes me inside her. She usually has an orgasm; when I have mine, I roll off her. We talk for a while and either duplicate the process or fall asleep in each other's arms.

And that's it. All of it. That's all she'll do. She won't suck me off or even take my cock in her mouth. She won't let me eat her or have anything to do with her rear end. And, of course, she'll have nothing to do with mine. She won't put her tongue in my mouth, and she certainly won't let me do this to her. She won't even put her hand on my cock, but she will let me manipulate her. She lets me suck her breasts, but from the way she stiffens when I do, I know she doesn't like it.

Before we got married, I had a very active sex life with a wide variety of partners. I think I know what most of the heterosexual possibilities are, and, at one time or another, I suppose I have tried them all and liked most of them. I miss them. I want her to suck me off. I want her ass once in a while. I'd like it dog fashion, and with her on top facing me, sometimes, and sometimes with her back to me, and spoon fashion, and all the other ways that people have sex.

I've asked her and asked her and asked her and she's been turning me down for years.

So I have fantasies. I have them when we are driving together in the car. The fantasy goes like this:

We are driving in the car, a station wagon. It's a fine clear night. The children are asleep in the back. The radio plays soft music. The traffic is light. My wife sits on the seat beside me. She's close to me. I can smell her hair and feel the warmth of her. I touch her leg with my hand and move it over her thighs. I run my hand up her thigh and rest it on her panties. She spreads her legs for me and I stroke her gently there until she begins getting moist. She raises up in the seat and pulls her panties off to give me easier access to her. When she sits back down, she comes down on my fingers that are waiting for her. They slip easily inside her and she smiles and reaches over and touches my fly, knowing exactly what she will find there. She strokes me through my pants a couple of times and opens up my fly and takes my cock in her hand and caresses it slowly up and down.

She gets up and turns around in the seat and checks to see that the kids are asleep. They are. She reaches behind the seat and picks up the blanket we keep there. While she is doing this, I am still running my fingers in and out of her and playing with her clit. I also get her ass wet with her juices. When she decides that the kids are all good and asleep, she turns around again and sits on my hand again. With my fingers in her cunt, her ass is in just the right position to massage. I do this while my fingers keep the juices flowing. In a minute or so, when she's ready, she raises up a little. I stiffen my thumb under her and she sinks down on it until it is as high in her ass as I can get.

She lies down on the seat, all curled up so I can keep my thumb and fingers in her without reaching. She puts her head in my lap and my cock in her mouth. My hand goes faster and faster inside her. I love the feeling of being able to feel my fingers with my thumb and the thumb with my fingers through the wall that separates them. She loves the feeling, too. She has told me this in words. Now she tells me with her body. She wriggles with pleasure all over the seat and sucks me with all her strength and skill. When I start coming, she sucks all the harder. She loves the taste of me and doesn't want to miss a drop.

My cock goes limp and she knows that for a little while it will be so sensitive, I will not want her to suck. So she just keeps her head where it is and holds me tenderly in her mouth. In a little while, my cock comes back to life again. She begins sucking very softly and my fingers and thumb begin working again. This time I work her to orgasm with my hand. When it's approaching, she begins sucking harder and harder. When I explode into her mouth, the thrill my coming gives her drives her over the edge. She soaks my hand with her fluids and sucks me till I have no more to give her.

She goes to sleep holding me in her mouth.

I once lived with a woman who liked sex in a way that I had never heard of and have experienced only with her. I liked it. I hope it doesn't sound disgusting. Making it explicit in words probably will make it sound terrible. But the actuality was not terrible. It was loving and tender and good and I think about it often and wish my wife would consent to it. Hell, I wish she'd ask for it.

She would go into the john and douche herself thoroughly, both anally and vaginally. When she climbed in bed a few minutes later, we would have all three kinds of sex: oral, anal, and genital. There was no set pattern to our lovemaking. Sometimes she'd want to start with my going down on her. Sometimes she'd go down on me first. Sometimes we'd sixty-nine it. Sometimes she'd say, "Start off in my ass, please." And sometimes she would leave the starting place up to me. Wherever we started, she would tell me after a moment or so where she wanted my cock in her next.

Because of the many, many pauses in this kind of lovemaking, I could go a long, long time before coming. Particularly if I had had a couple of drinks. On a couple of occasions, we made love like this three times successively. When we were both rested enough to manage this, I would come in a different place each time.

I've known many women. Most have a preference for one kind of sex or another. They like, say, vaginal sex best, oral next, and anal last. Or some other order of preference. This lady liked all three best.

Wouldn't it be fine if my wife read this book and recognized this part of it as my fantasy? But she won't. She wouldn't read a book like yours. * * * *

Alas.

SURPRISE!

* * * * I have been reading *Screw,* the sex industry's trade magazine, and I see a little ad for a girl who gives private massage. My wife is not due home for a couple of hours. The girl's telephone number is given in the ad, and I can tell from the exchange that she lives in the neighborhood. I call the number, a girl answers, and I ask her if I can have an appointment now. She gives me an address five or six blocks away.

I show up and ring the bell. A girl greets me at the door with her hat and coat on. She tells me Dolly is in the bathroom freshening up. She also tells me Dolly will show me a real good time. "Read a magazine or have a drink or something, she'll be out in a minute." Then she leaves.

I fix a drink and start getting turned on a little and think about the coincidence of the whore's name being Dolly and my wife's name being the same.

"Hello there, honey," this voice says behind me. I turn around and she's something to see. Low-cut gown that shows everything she's got; loads of sexy makeup; high, high heels. For a second we don't recognize each other. When we do, we both almost faint. To discover that your wife is a whore while you yourself are there to buy her services is a strange situation.

We brazened it out. I laid her, paid her, and returned home. She arrived a while later, dressed normally. We had friends coming for dinner. The evening went without incident. After they left, we went to bed and made love. I left for work as usual the next day and so did she. Before the discovery, we never talked much about our occupations. We still don't.

I visit her professionally now and don't use the services of other whores. She does things when I pay her that I never even dreamed she knew about—Greek and French. She doesn't do these things at home. Our marriage is better. She doesn't have to tell any more lies and I get the kick of going to a whorehouse without being sneaky about it.

The only uncomfortable thing I find in all this is the money. She left a savings book out once where I could see it. In our joint savings account we have a little under $19,000. In her professional account, she has about $100,000 more than that.

I fantasize all the time about what she is doing with her customers. I visit her on the days when the fantasies are most vivid. What a funny world this is. * * * *

Can you guess whether this is a fantasy or not? I can't. I met this man at a party. I was also introduced to his wife. I was dying to verify his story with her but I was too chicken to walk over and ask a perfect stranger whether she was a whore or not. Are you waiting for the line, "Well she certainly didn't act like a whore?" You'll wait a long time. I've met a number of whores. Some are very pleasant people. And some, of course, are not.

CHOPPING ONIONS

* * * * My girl is in the kitchen chopping something. Onions, probably. I can hear the chop, chop, chop, and although I can't see her, I know her boobs are bouncing up and down as she chops and her ass is wiggling. If I weren't so chicken, I'd go in there, lift her skirts, and stick it in her from behind, without taking her panties off, to increase the friction. * * * *

PLEASE

* * * * We were all in the living room, drunk. It was about ten

o'clock at night and we'd been drinking steadily since about five. I had bought a copy of *Playgirl* that afternoon and we had been looking at the pictures. My wife and Ed and I were interested in the nude photographs of male movie stars and their big, half-erect schlongs. But we were not sexually aroused by them. Mary Ann was.

We put the magazine aside and continued drinking and talking and playing the piano and singing, and suddenly Mary Ann grabbed me and French-kissed me. She had been sitting beside me on the sofa. She was suddenly on her knees between my legs groping around in my crotch. "I want to blow you. I'm going to suck you off."

I took her hands away and told her I thought Ed, six feet away playing the piano and watching us with a drunken grin, would object. Even though I was holding her hands, she now had her head buried in my crotch and was trying to suck me off through my pants. She raised her head up for a moment to say, "Fuck Ed. I'll blow who I want to blow." She buried her head in my lap again.

"Well, if Ed doesn't object, I'm sure Nancy will," I said. Nancy's my wife. She was standing beside Ed at the piano glaring at us. "Fuck her, too," Mary Ann said, her voice coming out muffled. "Well, if you blow me, then Nancy should blow Ed. Fair's fair." Nancy looked at me with horror.

Mary Ann took her head out of my crotch. She is the world's most jealous woman. If Ed even talks to another woman for more than a few minutes, Mary Ann creates a scene. The thought of him being blown by Nancy was too much for her. She got unsteadily to her feet and apologized to us all. She put her arms around Ed and said, "It's that goddamned magazine. Please forgive me. I just got carried away."

We continued drinking and singing for another couple of hours. Mary Ann behaved herself. After they left, Nancy told me I had handled the situation well. She was curious. Had Mary Ann aroused me? I never lie to her. I told her yes. She dragged me into the bedroom and blew me. She later told me that what Mary Ann had done had excited her greatly and she had spent the remainder of the evening hoping they would leave so she could get me in her mouth.

Mary Ann called me the next day to thank me for the nice time she and Ed had had. I asked her if she remembered anything unusual about the evening. She said no. I told her what she had done. She said, "Oh my God how awful," and hung up. About a half hour later, after having verified what I told her with Ed, she called back. She said she was sober now and she still wanted to blow me. "When you and Nancy started living together years ago, she told me how much she liked you in her mouth. She said you had the most suckable cock she had ever sucked. I've dreamed about blowing you since then. I'm sure I'll never get you in my mouth. If I did, I'd never be able to face Nancy again. But I still want to suck you off. If you asked me to come down right now, I'd be in a cab like a shot."

She paused, waiting for the invitation, I guess. "Would you throw me out if I came down now?" she asked. I'm only human, after all. I told her to get down here as fast as she could. Thinking about being in her mouth had given me a hard on. She arrived in about a half an hour and blew me twice. I have never told Nancy and she has never told Ed. We all continue to see each other and enjoy each other's company. She comes down here two or three times a month to blow me. We've never had sex in any other way. Once Ed and Nancy passed out at her house and she blew me there, right on her living room floor. I don't understand it. But I love it. And I think about it often, especially when Nancy is sucking me off, and most especially when she sucks me off on the same day Mary Ann has. I'm thinking about it now. I've never called her to ask her to blow me. I think I will.

She's on the way. * * * *

It is impossible to tell if this is a recollective fantasy or a flight of erotic imagination. I rather suspect the former because of the frequency of the writer's use of the first person singular. This is exactly the kind of fantasy, it seems to me, that would appeal to a man with a well-developed ego, an ego impelling him to believe he is irresistible to the women he knows. There is a mental disorder called "erotomania" in which the sufferer imagines that all women find him irresistible. It is a disease common to rapists. The rapist believes he is having normal sex with a willing partner. It is unimaginable to him that any woman would not like to have sex with him. Perhaps the man who reported this fantasy releases his erotomaniacal urges (if any) through his fantasy.

MY SECRETARY

    * * * * I think about this one often. It never fails to arouse me. I was thinking about it one day and became beautifully erect. My wife saw my erection and asked me what I was thinking about. I told her and it aroused her, too. I lied to her however. I told her it was pure (or impure, if you will) fantasy and that it never really happened. But it did really happen. And am I glad. It's the sexiest thing that ever happened to me. It's the sexiest thing I ever heard. Just thinking about it and writing about it has me aroused now. I hope you don't mind being written to by a man with a hard on. I'll bet when you're through reading this, you'll have a hard on, too.

If you have a wife, I suggest you show this to her. If it works for yours like it works for mine, I guarantee you'll get laid.

Here goes:

I'm a PR man with an agency. I went to work for a large New York-based firm in its San Francisco office. I met my new secretary the first day on the job. She was young, tiny, dark, small-titted, pretty, and bright. The head of the office introduced us. It was lust at first sight for both of us.

I had never cheated on my wife until this girl. I have never cheated with anybody else except this girl.

After I had been introduced to everybody in the office, I went into my own office to do some dictating. Patty came in and sat down primly with a pencil and steno pad. While she took down what I was saying, she never once looked at the pad. Her eyes never left my crotch. My office was small and we were sitting almost knee to knee. Every now and then she would look into my eyes to make sure I knew where she was looking. I let her know I knew in a reasonably obvious way. I got a hard on like a baseball bat, a real throbber.

When I finished dictating, she leaned over close to me, her head close to my cock, and said, in a small voice, "I hope you'll let me have that in my mouth some day." I think I said something like, "It's practically an inevitability."

About a week later I had to go to New York and Chicago. I figured I'd be gone for three days at the outside. I told my wife I'd be gone all week to give myself two or three days with Patty.

In bed, she was sensational. Even out of bed, she was sensational. I walked into her apartment. She was fixing martinis. She let me in, kissed me, and went right down on her knees in front of me. As she was going down, I was going up. She unzipped me with her teeth, pulled me out of my underwear, and started sucking. I came in five or ten seconds. When she got it all, she looked up at me with a sort of hurt look. "Can I do it again? I've been waiting for this for days and you came so fast. I want to suck it for a good long time."

I told her that it was so sensitive that if she even touched me with her tongue, it would hurt. Maybe in twenty minutes or so. We took our clothes off and had a martini. I had a second while she knelt between my legs and did it again. I'm really pretty good at holding myself back after I have come the first time and I told her this. She asked if I could hold off until she told me she had had enough. I told her I'd try. She sucked me for maybe fifteen minutes and then said, "May I have your milk now, please?" I came again for her in a minute or so.

After having dinner, we put the dishes in the dishwasher, turned out the lights, lit a candle, and went to bed. We made love once or twice, I think, and I went to sleep with my cock in her mouth. She told me, before we went to sleep, that she had slept with twenty-five men and had sucked them all off when they asked her. She never once liked it. I was the first man she had ever asked to suck off. It was the first time she enjoyed it.

My ego soared.

I woke up hours later. Her head was underneath the covers. She had a flashlight. She was looking at my cock. She had it between her fingers and was moving it this way and that, pulling the foreskin back to get a really close look. My cock was all wet. She said she had washed me with soap and water while I slept.

She told me that many men had tried to fuck her up the ass and she had always declined. "Will you do this for me someday but not now?" I told her my wife wouldn't let me do this, so I had never done it either. I told her yes, I'd like to.

We made love again. She washed me this time while I was awake. I got hard. She took me in her mouth and we slept again. When we awoke, she sucked me off, and then we went to work in separate cabs. We spent the next night together. It was very much like the first. She told me then that she had never had an orgasm in her life, but I had brought her the closest.

We spent at least one night a week together for the next several months. One night we had anal sex. She said she thought that if she masturbated herself while I fucked her in the ass, she might have an orgasm. Before the anal sex, we made love a couple of times to make sure I could fuck her a long time before I came. I fucked her for as long as I could last, maybe a half hour or so, before I shot my wad. Nothing for her. She decided she didn't like anal sex very much. I told her it really turned me on. "Then you can have it that way any time you want," she said.

A really fine lady, this secretary of mine.

She worried about the orgasm thing a lot and so did I. I really wanted her to have one with me. She had an idea one night, and we tried it out.

What she liked best, she said, was sucking me off. That gave her the best feeling, particularly when she masturbated herself. When I was not with her, she used to masturbate and suck on fat sausages and pretend they were me. She did this lying on her back in the bathtub, with tepid water running on her clitoris. With one hand she rubbed her clit and with the other she ran a hairbrush handle in and out of herself.

She said she thought that if she masturbated herself this way, while she was actually sucking on me instead of a sausage, she just might come.

It took her a long time to tell me this because she was embarrassed about telling me that she masturbated and how she did it.

I told her it sounded exciting as hell.

We went into the bathroom and she adjusted the water the way she liked it. She rolled up a towel for me to kneel on and put it crossways in the tub. Sitting on the edge of the tub, she sucked me off to make sure I could last a long time in her mouth. She got in the tub, moved her pussy so the water hit her the way that was best for her, and started masturbating. She was embarrassed to have me watch. But she got over it when I told her how nice it was to watch. After a little while, she told me to get in the tub with her and put it in her mouth.

I got in the tub and knelt on the towel and put it in her mouth. I don't know why I find this so exciting. She really took it deep. She pushed me away and told me not to just let her suck on me, but to pump in and out of her mouth, to fuck her in the mouth in other words. I told her that it might hurt her if I tried to get the whole thing in her mouth and down her throat.

We'd been making love together for a year or more at this point, and I thought I knew her pretty well. She blushed and said: "I feel like some kind of sickie or something and I hope you won't hate me after I've said this. I've been rehearsing the words for days." She paused, mustering her courage, then she finally blurted out (her words tumbling out in a rush so fast and so softly that they were hard to hear): "I want you to fuck me in the mouth. I want you to hurt me. If I tell you to stop, don't stop. Fuck me harder. Jam it all the way down my throat. Pretend you're raping me. If I try to push you off, pinion my arms. After you come, piss on me. Piss on my face and neck and hair. My mouth will be open for you. Fill it with piss, if you can. And while you're doing all this, while you're raping me and hurting me and humiliating me, I want you to call me filthy names. Cuntlapper, cocksucker, whore, asshole-fucker."

I was absolutely appalled. My erection disappeared, and I got out of the tub.

She began crying, and I got dressed and went home. When I saw her in the office the next day, she looked terrible. She told me later that she had cried all night and had thought about committing suicide. She would quit her job if I asked her, she said.

I told her I hadn't slept much that night myself. I told her I didn't think I could stand hurting her. Suppose, when she told me to stop, she really meant it, and I went on hurting her anyhow? How would I know if stop meant stop, in other words. She looked terribly relieved that I had been thinking about what she wanted and was not repelled. She explained that she didn't think the game would work unless she knew that I would not stop hurting her and cursing her, no matter what happened.

The next time we made love, we did it her way. When she tried to get me out of her mouth I pinned her arms. She tried to turn her head so my cock would come out, and I slapped her. I got everything I owned into her mouth and called her cocksucker every time I jammed myself into her. I came way down deep in her throat someplace and pulled out and pissed on her and in her mouth. Why the neighbors didn't show up in answer to her screams, I don't know. But she had her orgasm. She cried all night, but managed to tell me that she loved every second of it and wanted me to do it again the next time we made love.

I was home with my wife the next night and the phone rang. It was Patty. She had just masturbated in her usual way in the tub, she said, and she had had a glorious, glorious orgasm.

From this time until we broke up a year or so later, she had orgasms whether she sucked me off or had anal sex or sex in the usual way. I see her every couple of years. She kisses me and whispers "Thank you" in my ear.

Can you imagine what that girl did for my ego? * * * *

I'm glad she now has orgasms. I think it's interesting, fascinating even, the way she achieved her first one. Also queasy-making. However that may be, she has provided one man a recollective fantasy that he obviously enjoys.

TEACHER'S PET

This man claims to be a teacher who writes pornography on the side. He claims to have written under dozens of assumed names. He says he writes about one porno novel every two months and is paid $800 for each one. He has sex fantasies all the time, he says. When he has a memorable one, he puts it in a steno pad notebook. When he has a pad full of notes, that's enough material, he says, to begin on a new novel. His novels are shamefully bad, loaded with incident and detailed description but without much plot or characterization, he says.

Judging by his fantasy, I would hazard a guess that he is, in fact, a teacher. But he is probably not a writer. Nevertheless, in my opinion, he ought to be a writer and he ought to do porn. He has a flair for filth, an eye for dirty detail, and a grand ability for facile and tawdry invention.

* * * * I'm sitting in my office at school with a hard on. Julie Trimble just called me on the telephone. She said she had to see me right away. She sounded desperate. I'm her physics counselor, but she can't want to talk to me about that. Nobody gets desperate about physics.

I'd better adjust my fly so she can't see my cock bulging. When she comes in, I'll have to stand up. I'll hold some papers in front of my cock.

I remember Julie, three years ago, as a skinny sophomore with big tits, and I'm thinking about her now, full and rounded and juicy, with big tits and long mahogany hair with highlights of red when the sun shines on it. I've never fucked one of my students, but I'd like to fuck Julie so much I can almost come thinking about it. I've never been unfaithful to Gloria in the six years of our marriage. But if I could get into Julie, to hell with fidelity.

Gloria and I both teach here. We both teach physics. Julie, despite her sensational body, is a little dumb. Gloria is tutoring her in physics. The faculty members know that Gloria and I are married, but the students do not. The students know her as Miss McJagger and not as Mrs. Ted Calvin.

Julie comes into the room without knocking. Her eyes are wide with fright, her hair is mussed, and her expression is frightened. She looks around to see if anybody else is here. Satisfied that we are alone, she shuts the door and bursts into tears. What a swine I am for thinking of fucking this frightened creature. She has come to me for help and all I can think of is her body.

She comes over to my desk and sits down. She rocks back and forth in her woe, and her tits swing in her blouse. I pat her shoulder with my left hand and push down on my cock with my right. Her miniskirt is sliding up, and I can see her blue panties and the triangle of reddish fur they cover.

Her sobs subside and eventually stop. She adjusts her skirt and looks morosely at the floor. Whatever it is she is about to tell me will be difficult for her to say. She can't look at me. Suddenly she makes up her mind. She looks at me with her frightened green eyes, and the words tumble out in a torrent. If she stops talking, even for a second, she will not be able to finish.

"Oh, Mr. Calvin," she begins, "I am so ashamed and confused. I have to tell someone. I hope you won't hate me for what I have done or what was done to me. I didn't know what was happening. It's Miss McJagger. I have to tell you all of it or you won't believe me.

"She came to my house to tutor me this afternoon. We were working in the living room. My mother was talking to somebody on the phone and my little brother was watching TV with some of his friends and Miss McJagger couldn't concentrate with all the noise. She suggested that we go to my bedroom and shut the door in order to shut out the noise.

"When we got to the bedroom and shut the door, she did not spread her papers out on the desk. Instead, she put them on the bed and motioned me to sit on it with her. She sat very close to me, and while she talked about physics, she kept touching me. She patted my knee and caressed my hair and ran her fingers through it. She leaned into me while she talked, so she could feel my breast against hers and I could feel hers. She patted my knee and began rubbing it. Her hand crept up my thigh, higher and higher. She moved her body in sort of a circle, her nipple rubbing against mine. I became sort of hypnotized, I guess; I could hear what she was saying, but I could not understand the words.

"Her hand finally came to rest between my legs and she began rubbing me there. I should have taken her hand away, but she is an older woman and my tutor, and I thought that would be disrespectful. She began by rubbing softly, outside my panties, but when she felt me getting wet, she moved her hand inside the panties. She found my clitoris and began massaging it between her thumb and forefinger.

"With her other hand, she began touching and kneading my breasts. First one, then the other. She massaged my nipples until they got hard. When they did, she reached up my back and unsnapped my bra and pushed my blouse up. She began kissing and sucking my breasts. I knew what she was doing was wrong. I knew that letting her do it was wrong. But I somehow could not help letting her rub me and suck me. I have never felt anything like what she was doing to me. She seemed to know exactly what my body wanted, she seemed to know all the places to touch and exactly how to touch them.

"As if in a dream, I found myself standing up. She knelt on the floor in front of me and pulled down my panties. She kissed me between my legs and licked me there. It felt so good, I whimpered. I guess she knew by then that she could do anything she liked with me. She took off her panties and put my hand between her legs. She unhooked her bra and pulled my head down to her breast."

My God! She's telling me my wife is a lesbian and I don't even care. While she's talking to me, her dress has moved up again and I can see the divine delta of her wonderful pubic hair. I stop pushing my hard on down and take my hand away from it. I don't care now if she sees my fly bulging out. In fact I want her to see it. I can tell that the telling of her story in all its details has gotten her aroused. Her panties are dark with her juices and her breasts are standing proud and firm. The nipples strain against her bra. I feel my cock against my leg. There's a little spot of dampness on my pants. If she keeps talking like this, I'll come. I won't be able to help myself. I'd love to suck her pussy while she's talking.

"I've never had sex with a woman. In fact I've never had sex with anybody. I didn't know exactly what was expected of me. But my body seemed to know what to do, what she wanted me to do. Oh, I'm so ashamed now. I'm so ashamed because I liked what she was doing to me with her hands and her mouth, and I liked what I was doing to her. I sucked her nipples and nibbled on them with my teeth. I knew she loved what I was doing. I could feel it in the wetness between her legs.

"She had her fingers in me and I had mine in her. With one hand she rubbed my clitoris, and with the other she pushed her fingers in and out of me. I have never felt anything like this in my life. It's so good. So good.

"We were lying on the bed, side by side. She stopped sucking on my breasts. She got off the bed and knelt on the floor. She put my legs over her shoulders and buried her head between my legs. What she did to me then was so good I can't describe it to you. She seemed to be able to do everything a vagina wants done to it all at once. I've never been so wet in my life. I looked down at her once and her face was all wet with my fluids and her saliva. It was actually dripping off her chin, and her hair was all matted and wet, and the room was filled with my smells and hers. While she was doing this to me, I saw she had her hand between her legs and was rubbing herself and putting all four fingers into herself."

Well, I thought, that clinches it. Julie's not making this up. That's how Gloria masturbates. I've watched her do it with all four fingers in her while she sucks me off.

"Her tongue was inside me. She sucked on my clitoris. She licked my bottom. She held my clitoris in her teeth and pulled on it lightly, in a way that made me cry out with happiness. It felt so good what she was doing to me that my head was going from side to side, and I was biting my lips to keep from crying out. My hands, without my willing them to, were holding her head and pulling her into me so that her tongue could get inside me deeper and the pressure on my clitoris would be greater. I loved it.

"I've had erotic dreams, so I know what it's like to have an orgasm. But I wasn't prepared for the one I had then. During a dream, the orgasm comes on quickly and lasts for just a second or so, until you wake up and then it goes away. But this one was different. It started slowly and built slowly, and then I started coming. I came in spasms that started out small, then grew and grew and, finally, erupted like an explosion. My whole body went rigid. My pelvis was grinding into her face, and my hands pulled her into me with all my strength. I don't know how she could breathe. But she kept on licking and sucking and biting and tonguing until the last of the spasms stopped.

"She seemed to know that it was all over for me except the

wonderful feeling of relaxation. She rested her head against my thigh and waited for both of us to catch our breath.

"Good as what she had just done to me was, what came next was better. She took my legs off her shoulders and put them on the floor. She crawled on top of me and straddled my face and slowly came down on it."

That's just what she does with me, I thought. She says she likes to sit on my face because she can move herself around so that my tongue is doing to her exactly what she wants it to do, in exactly the right spot and at exactly the right pressure. When I'm doing this to her, she talks to me. She tells me what she wants done in detail. When she talks to me like this, it really turns me on.

"She started talking to me, and she kept calling me Ted for some reason. She told me what to suck and lick and bite and tongue. She told me how to do it, how hard to do it. When she moved her pelvis forward, my tongue got into her deep, and when she moved it back, her clitoris went into my mouth. I was masturbating while I was eating her. I did what I had seen her do, except I could only get one finger inside myself. I had never masturbated before and I loved the feeling. I wished I were bigger down there because I'm sure more fingers would give more feeling. I kneaded my clit and shot my fingers in and out, and I don't know which I liked better, eating her or masturbating me. I loved both. I adored both.

"She tasted so good and her vagina was so lovely and big. When she squatted down on me, my lips and nose would go inside her and I would get this lovely feeling of almost drowning inside her. I found myself doing impossible things. I licked, sucked, bit, and moved my head in circles, just as she had done to me. She, I had thought, had had a lot of practice. But I don't know. Maybe not. I was doing everything she did to me and doing it just as well, I think . . . I *know* . . . just as well as she did.

"When she came, it was absolutely divine. Her vagina got bigger and wetter, and I could actually feel the spasms in my mouth. She twitched, her vagina got big, then smaller, then bigger again. Her fluids poured into my mouth, and I drank them because they tasted so good.

Thinking about how good I was making her feel made me come at the same time she did. My spasms matched hers. I could feel my spasms with my fingers and I knew that if mine felt as good as hers, she was in heaven with me.

"She got off me after a while and we both got dressed and she left. I took a little nap. What we had both been doing was hard work and I needed rest. As I fell asleep, I was smiling and remembering how good it had been. But when I woke up, I was disgusted with myself. I had just discovered that I am a lesbian, and I don't want to be one. Someday I want to get married to a nice man and give him a lot of beautiful babies. I don't want to be a lesbian. Oh, Mr. Calvin, what am I going to do? Can you help me?"

During the last few minutes, while she was talking to me, I had gotten so worked up that I was pacing up and down in back of my desk with my cock sticking out about a foot in front of me. I didn't realize I was doing it. When she finishes talking, I stop pacing and come to a stop in front of her. My fly is bulging inches from her nose. She stares at my fly with a look that combines both fright and wonderment. I guess she has never seen an erection before. She looks up at me in confusion. She raises her hand to touch my fly but can't bring herself to do it. I'm twenty-nine, more than ten years older than she is, and she's shy.

I make her stand up, when actually what I want to do is unzip and plunge into her mouth. (I don't do this. It might frighten her.) I raise her lips to mine. Her lips are full and red and bruised from what she had been doing with my wife earlier in the day. Gloria's smell lingers. Julie's eyes are shut. Her breasts rise and fall passionately as she waits for my kiss.

Lightly at first, and then with increasing pressure, I kiss her. I force her mouth open with my tongue and explore the inside of her mouth. At first, she does not respond. Then her tongue finds mine and moves enthusiastically around it. It darts in and out of my mouth like a little bird. She tastes marvelous.

My arms are around her holding her close to me. Involuntarily, I have shoved my pelvis into her and she can feel my cock against her. She likes it and is excited by it. Her hips move back and forth and make a slow, voluptuous circle at the same time.

We break apart, and she turns her back on me to have me undo her bra. I reach up under her blouse and unsnap it. She turns around again and faces me. I take one tit in each hand and rub and squeeze them gently. She looks into my eyes. She likes what I am doing, but she can't believe I'm doing it. Her breasts are huge and firm. The nipples are hard with their wanting. They want me to inflame them. I walk her over to the couch and take the blouse off. The nipples are large and the areola is pink. I suck her tits and nibble them. While I suck one, I massage the other. She has her hand between her legs and is rubbing herself. I take her hand away gently and replace it with my own. I put my fingers inside her panties and rub her wet pussy. She shoves herself forward so that my finger goes inside her. She's tight in there. I wonder if my large cock will hurt her. She's so hot that her pussy is sucking on my finger. I take her panties off. She's sopping wet, and her pussy shines pinkly through the matted hair. I put my tongue in it, and she tastes new and young and fresh and fine. She starts whispering my name over and over again and her hips roll as I lick her pussy and suck her little, hard clit. She sits on the desk and puts her legs around my neck and thrusts at me to get me in deeper. She's inexperienced, but she's learning fast. While I eat her pussy, I'm fondling her breasts. Her head rolls from side to side while she whispers my name. Her eyes are squeezed shut. She opens her eyes and looks at me tonguing her. I like her looking at me.

I stand up and drop my pants and kick off my shoes. I drop my shorts and my cock flies up and slaps me on the belly. The head of it is swollen and purple and wet. I forget that she is just a child who has never had a man before. I kneel over her and offer her my cock to suck. She takes it in her mouth like she was born to it. Her teeth hurt me, and I tell her not to bite but to suck and suck hard. Suck the head, I tell her, and then go as far down the shaft as you can and then go slowly back up the shaft to the head again, sucking all the way. I tell her that I am so hot that I am going to come in just a second. I tell her I am really going to shoot hard into her mouth and she'll probably gag. That's normal, I say, the first time a girl sucks a man off. Swallow my sperm, I tell her. It will taste a little salty, but you'll like it.

God, I come like a stud horse. She gags and gags, and the sperm leaks out around the side of her mouth and dribbles down her chin, but she's a good girl and keeps on sucking and swallowing, despite her discomfort. It's such a pretty sight, my cock in this beautiful child's mouth. I get carried away and start thrusting hard into her mouth as I come. I feel myself bumping against the back of her throat. She doesn't know yet how to get the entire length down. I'll explain it to her later.

I come and come and come and, when I finish, my cock stays hard. I try to pull it out of her mouth, but she wants to keep sucking it. "Don't take it away from me," she says when I get it out, "I want to keep sucking it forever."

I tell her I'm going to do something to her she'll like even more.

I know she's a virgin and I must be gentle with her. I go down on her and give her a good lick to make her nice and wet for me. Unnecessary. She's soaking. I spread her legs and get the head of my cock against her. She's looking at me, wide-eyed. I ease into her gently until my cock comes to rest on her maidenhead, just inside her. I ease back slowly. She tells me to break it. It will hurt, I tell her, easing back in her slowly. She bucks against me and gives a little gasp of pleasure and pain, and my cock slides in to the hilt.

She's like a wild woman. She doesn't know anything about the rhythms of sex or about working together with her partner. She wriggles and squirms and bumps against me with all her strength. She loves the cock in her and she loves it in all the way. I tell her to stop all the gyrating around. I tell her to lie still. She looks at me, puzzled, but she does what she's told.

I start fucking her, in and out, in and out, slowly at first, then picking up speed. She gets the idea. When I thrust, she thrusts; when I pull back, she pulls back. At the end of just a minute or so, she's fucking me like she's been doing it all her life.

She's so tight that I can feel myself building to an orgasm. I can tell it's really going to be something special. She throws her arm across her mouth to keep herself from screaming. She makes guttural, animal noises way back in her throat, and my cock feels her strong rhythmic pulsings. She sucks my cock with her cunt, her whole being yearns for my sperm. I hold back, still thrusting into her as fast as I can go. Her orgasm builds and builds. She's gasping with pleasure. She's holding onto both my arms with all her strength, thrusting at me with youthful abandon. When she climaxes, it's a joy to see. Her back is arched and her teeth are clenched and her mouth is drawn back, as if she is experiencing extreme pain. The orgasm subsides, and her rhythms slow down, and I come. I don't come as I did in her mouth, I come even more. I can feel the stuff flying out of me. I feel it streaming into her, filling her and gushing out of her and wetting my balls that are banging her wet, tight little ass.

Then it is all over. I fall on top of her, exhausted, with my cock diminishing inside her and finally falling out. My head is on her breast, which is still rising and falling as she gasps for air. I get off her and take the handkerchief out of the breast pocket of my jacket and clean my bloody cock off. I spread her limp legs a little and wipe the sperm and blood that bubble out.

I put my clothes back on, and she does the same. Neither of us says a word. When we're dressed, I take her in my arms and kiss her gently on the lips and downcast eyes.

"Did you like sex with me or with Gloria best?" I ask her.

"I liked it with you best, Mr. Calvin. I'll never have sex with another woman after this. I'm glad you have shown me I'm not a lesbian but a real woman. If you'll let me, I will come to you every afternoon. I want to drink your come every day and feel you squirting inside me. I don't know whether I like sucking you or fucking you best, but I want both every day."

"Tomorrow afternoon I don't teach," I tell her, "Come to my apartment at around two, and we can spend the afternoon together. I'll teach you things you've never dreamed of, things as good as fucking and sucking. And, if you like, Gloria can join us. I like to watch women making love to each other, particularly Gloria. She's my wife and we do threesomes every chance we get." * * * *

It took "Ted" possibly forty minutes to tell me all this. He spoke slowly, obviously making it up as he went along. I think it's vivid and real and trashy, and probably salable as hard-core porn. If you're reading this, Ted, take my advice and chuck teaching, or whatever you do, and grind out pornography.

PIERCE HIGH

* * * * My wife and I teach at Pierce High (not its name, of course, but appropriate). Occasionally, one of us will seduce a student and tell the other about it. She has relations with both boys and girls. I am totally heterosexual.

We've caught each other several times and don't bother to lie about what we're doing. I'm sure there are many rumors about us among the students. As long as faculty and parents don't hear them, it's fine with us. Our reputations bring the horny students to us, which is a perfect arrangement.

Last year, my wife walked into my office at school at an awkward moment. I was seated at my desk, and kneeling in the well of the desk was one of my prettier students. She was gnawing away on my joint. Just as my wife walked in, I came, and the girl gagged. When I was finished coming, my wife told the girl to get out of there. The ladies faced each other and began giggling. I realized that the student and my wife had had sex together. My wife locked the office door and took her panties off. She put her hands on the student's shoulders and the girl willingly went to her knees and began lapping. Naturally, this excited me, and I asked my wife to suck me off. She said she'd rather have it up the ass.

There was no KY Jelly or Vaseline in the office and, because her ass is very tight, she needs lubrication before I can enter her there. I knelt behind her and spread her buns and made her wet with my tongue. I stood up and pushed my penis through her legs and the girl licked the head of it. I got into her easily. When I thrust forward, my balls thumped against the girl's mouth and chin and, every thrust or so, she'd give them a nice lick. My wife and I came, and the student, after having blown me and eaten my wife, needed release in the worst (best) way. Classes were over for the day, so we all went home together. I drove and the two of them got in the back of the panel truck and pulled the curtains. I asked them what they were going to do. They discussed it for a few minutes and decided on two vibrators for the girl, while my wife sat on her face with a third vibrator in her anus.

We were out of the town now and it was safe to make noise. The girls were screaming with pleasure.

We walked into the house and dropped our clothes just inside the door and decided to take a shower together. Both ladies still had the anal vibrators in and working. They presented me their rears, and I removed the vibrators and turned them off. We got into the tub and peed on each other. The girl had never seen people do this before. She bent over and stuck her tongue into the stream coming out of me. She giggled and said she liked it. She washed my front while I washed hers and my wife did my back. I washed my wife while the girls douched each other and gave each other enemas. My wife sucked me off while the girl gave me my enema. Then we washed each other's feet and got out of the tub.

I didn't feel like sex, having had three orgasms in an hour and a half or so. The girls went to the bedroom. I fixed myself a drink and went in to watch them. They played sixty-nine and worked on each other furiously with dildos. After a while we feared the girl's parents might worry about her whereabouts, so I drove her home. She sucked me all the way, but I was unable to come for her. My wife brought me off when I got home. She's not as vigorous at cocksucking as the student, but she's more experienced and knows better what I like. When she sucks me, she puts her finger a little way up my ass and twists her finger in there. She can make me come this way at times when I don't even think it's possible for me to get an erection.

That student, by the way, visited my office every school day until she graduated at the end of the year. She never once let me into her vagina. At that time, nothing had been in there except fingers, tongues, vibrators, and dildos. Being in the well of my desk with my cock in her mouth thrilled her, she said. The first boy she blew—I was the first person she ever sucked off and I'll tell you about that first time in a minute—she blew in her parents' living room. She had him sit at her father's desk and she crawled into the well.

I teach English, as I suppose you have surmised from the way I write, and this girl was having a bad time with grammar. She spoke and wrote well, but the intricacies of sentence structure and the parts of speech eluded her. Since she was a senior and needed to pass my course, sophomore English, which she had taken and flunked two years before, I suggested tutorial sessions with me after school. I was not thinking about sex with her. I was genuinely trying to help her pass the course.

She came every afternoon after class, and we worked together for about an hour. One day, unaccountably, she did not show up. I asked her about it the next day. She blushed beet red to the roots of her hair, as they say, and said she had been delayed. Since what delayed her caused her embarrassment, I did not pursue the matter. We launched into the day's lesson for which she was totally unprepared, something that had not occurred before. I terminated the lesson and told her to come back when she had done her homework. The lesson now being at an end, I expected her to gather up her books and leave, but she seemed inclined to stay and talk. She was an intelligent kid and interesting to talk to. She was also an avid reader, so we talked about books.

Someone had recently given her a copy of the *The Story of O*. She had never read pornography before—if *O* is pornography. I happen to think it's art, myself, and trust you agree. She found it "most stimulating." At this point, she began blushing again. At the end of my wife's class with her, she, my wife, noticed the book under her arm as the girl was going out of the room. My wife stopped her and they started talking about the book.

With a lot of "ums" and "ers" and with a heaving bosom—as the trashy novelists would say—she told me that my wife had put her hand up her skirt and into her panties and had rubbed her there until she was so excited she forgot to come to the office for her lesson. She went directly home, she said. From her blushes, I imagine she finished at home what my wife had begun at school. I asked her if she wanted me to report my wife to the principal. She said no. She said my wife had asked her if I ever touched her there and she told her the truth, which was no. She said my wife said, "You ought to let him. It's lovely and soft." She was staring at her feet in great embarrassment as she related this little story to me.

I asked her what she thought of my wife's suggestion. She shook her head and said nothing. I asked her if she would like me to touch her where my wife had touched her. She didn't answer in words. She just stood up and came over to my side of the desk and stood there waiting. I told her to go over and lock the door and turn out the lights so people would think the office was empty. She did what I asked and came back and stood mutely where she had stood before. I told her not to be nervous or embarrassed and that to want to be touched there was perfectly natural and normal. I asked if she was a virgin. She nodded yes. I asked if she had ever touched herself there and received another nod. Then I told her that she must know that I could touch her better if she'd let me take her panties off. She moved closer to my chair and I slowly and gently took them off. She was glistening and wet.

I was very gentle. I touched her softly on the outside. She shuddered when my hand first touched her and I began rubbing gently. After a few moments, she spread her legs slightly and began moving herself back and forth on my hand and squatting down a bit to increase the pressure. I asked her if I could put a finger in, and she said yes. I told her after a few seconds of this that I thought it would be better for her if I put in two fingers or possibly three. She agreed.

I was, of course, erect and had been for some time. By this time, I had swivelled my chair around to face her. She could see my bulging fly. I asked her if she would like to see a man's penis and if she had ever seen one before. She said she had seen her father's penis a few times but nobody else's. I loosened my belt and undid my pants and pulled them down a little so she could see all of me. "It's so big," she said. I told her that while my fingers were inside her, she could touch me if she liked. I told her men are extremely tender there and her touch should be extremely gentle and tender. She began caressing me gently and had her first orgasm. She did not take her hand off me, but she asked me to take my fingers out of her for a few minutes.

"Some of my girl friends tell me that, to cool their boyfriends off, they give head. I would like to do it to you but I couldn't bear to have you watch me do it. Will you let me do it and not watch? Can I get under the desk so you can't watch me even if you wanted to?"

I told her yes and moved the chair so she could get in the well.

"I've heard all about what men taste like," she said. "I mean I know that your penis will taste salty and that your sperm is thick and hot and salty. My girl friends drink it and say it's a wonderful taste. Can I drink yours?"

I told her yes, and she got under the desk between my legs and took me in her mouth. I warned her that she had excited me so much that I was going to come almost immediately. She sucked on me for just a matter of seconds and I came.

She told me her girl friends had told her the truth. It was a wonderful taste and a wonderful sensation to suck a man. She said she wished that it had lasted longer. I told her that if she waited a few minutes, she could do it again and I would last much longer and could hold off until she told me she'd had enough. She stayed under the desk fondling me until I began to get erect again. I let her suck me until the end of my wife's last class.

I told her to suck harder so I could give her more to drink. With my cock still in her mouth, she shook her head vigorously from side to side. She wasn't ready for me to come yet. I lied and said I couldn't last any longer. I came and it was better than the first time. I got a little carried away, in fact, during that orgasm. My pelvis was moving violently and banging her head against the bottom of the desk's middle drawer. She was so interested in what she was doing that she didn't stop and brought me off in fine fashion.

While she was putting on her panties, and I was adjusting my trousers, she told me she loved giving me head and would like to do it every day. Twice. Once the fast way and once the long way. If I could manage it, she would like me to last much longer tomorrow than I had today. I told her I would try. I also told her to come with her lessons prepared.

We walked out of the building together. She walked me to the van and said goodnight to both my wife and me. While I was starting the car, my wife gave me a sly look and asked how the lesson went. I gave her all the details as we drove, just as I have given them to you here. Telling her excited her, and she vibrated herself to several climaxes as I drove. We had fine sex when we got home. I fucked her, and while we fucked, we used vibrators on each other.

The final thing I want to tell you is this: I don't teach English or anything else. I don't fuck anybody but my wife. She doesn't fuck anybody but me. What I have written is pure fantasy. And speaking of fucking my wife, I think I will end this and take care of that little matter right now.

I'm back after having completed the deed mentioned above. While I'm typing this, my bride is reading what I have written. She says it's the horniest stuff she has ever read. She also says that when she's finished reading, she wants me to fuck her again.

I'm glad I saw your ad. It has made my whole day, for which I thank you kindly. And my wife does, too. * * * *

THE ESCOFFIER OF THE IND

* * * * I'm riding on the IND. There's just me and two fine foxes in the car. I take my clothes off so they can see what a fine body I've got. I see the conductor calling the Transit Authority cops, the son of a bitch. He comes into the car with his fucking two-foot stick, and just as one of the girls is about to blow me, he rams the stick up my ass. He watches the girl suck me off while he runs the stick in and out of my ass.

I'm at my girl's house. She's stirring pancake mix with a wire whisk. I tell her that's no way to stir pancake mix. She starts licking my cock. I get hard and shove it into her ass a few times. Then I put it in the mix and stir it up. After I come in the mix, she makes pancakes. She says from now on she'll never have them any other way. She sucks the mix off my joint. She says that's fine, too. * * * *

I THINK ABOUT IT BEFORE I GET DOWN TO IT

This one came from an Air Force brigadier general. I wonder how the officers and men in his command would react if, just for the sport of the thing, I put his name in here.

* * * * Oddly enough, I don't feel embarrassed about telling you this fantasy at all. I've told it to my wife and it amuses her. I had to tell her to explain why I wear a jockstrap all the time. If I didn't wear it, everybody would know that about ninety percent of the time I have a hard on. Not a little hard on, but a great big throbbing motherfucker. I come in my pants a couple of times a year having this fantasy of mine. I wouldn't part with it for another star.

Whenever I see a woman, any woman from nine to ninety, fat or skinny, black or white, beautiful or ugly, I picture myself eating her. I picture all the details. Parting the lips with my fingers, finding the clitoris with my tongue, sucking and nibbling on it till her juices and mine are running down my chin. I've got this fantasy down so pat that my mouth actually waters and I can taste the tastes and smell the smells. Gee, it's nice.

When this part of the fantasy is over, I see the same woman blowing me. She gets down on her knees in front of me and undoes my fly. She pulls down the jockstrap and takes my cock, which is pretty big, into her mouth. All the cocksuckers in my fantasies are fantastic. They get the whole thing in their mouths and just suck away on it as if their lives depended on giving me the best blow job I've ever had. They make loud sucking noises. They really gobble like they love the work. When I come, it's a much bigger deal than in real life. The woman gags and chokes, and she can't get all the sperm down. She has come on her lips when she's through. She wipes it off with the back of her hand. She thanks me and asks if I've had enough. She'll do it again for me if I want her to because mine is the nicest cock it has been her privilege to suck.

I always have this fantasy just before I get down to it. My wife and I are the two best fed people in the Air Force. * * * *

MY LIFE IS A LITTLE COMPLICATED

I had a little trouble understanding this caller. He's a South

American and has been in the country less than a year. He says he is twenty-five, has a college degree, is married, and his wife is pregnant. How much of what he reports and how much is imagination, I can't guess. If it's all fact, you have to admire his stamina.

* * * * My life is a little complicated. As my wife's belly gets bigger and bigger, she likes to fuck less and less. I am a normal man and I need to fuck. I have been fucking since I was seventeen. Before I got to this country I thought all there was to sex was fucking. Recently, I have begun to learn better.

There is a pretty young girl who works where I work. We take our coffee breaks together. Sometimes we eat lunch together. I told her that my wife wouldn't let me fuck her as much as I like. The girl told me to come to her house that night. I went to her house and we fucked. I go to her house every night and we fuck two or three times. The girl is very noisy when we fuck. One night I was fucking her and her mother came home unexpectedly. Her mother actually came into the room where we were fucking. I saw her but her daughter did not. Mama smiled and seemed happy we were having such a good time. The next day Mama called me on the phone at work. She asked me to come and see her. She wanted to speak to me. It is no problem for me to leave my work. I went to her house. I was not afraid because I knew she was not angry.

I rang the doorbell and Mama let me in. She led me into the living room. Her dress fell off and she was standing there naked. My penis got hard because she has a beautiful body. She has very small breasts with large pink nipples. These are the kinds of breasts I like. I thought she wanted me to fuck her. She did not. She pulled my penis out and put it in her mouth. No one had ever done that before. It felt so good that I began yelling. I don't know why, but I yelled, "Mama, Nancy, Nancy, Mama," over and over again. When I came, it was the best feeling I have ever had, much better than fucking.

Mama fixed me some coffee. I sat down in a chair to drink it. She came over to me and took the coffee away and put her pussy in my face. She told me to lick her. Her pussy smelled good so I licked her. Her pussy is very large and wet. It tasted good. She told me to press into her hard and to suck her pussy, too. Her pussy got bigger and bigger, and I pressed into her harder and harder. I got my whole head in. I couldn't breathe, but it was very nice. After a while she told me to stop. She lay down on the floor on her back. She told me to kneel on top of her with my head between her legs and my penis near her mouth. She pushed my head between her legs and she put my penis in her mouth. She sucked me and I sucked her and it was very nice and I came very fast.

Now every day I go see Mama, and every night I go see her daughter. Every day Mama sucks me two or three times and I suck her. Every night I fuck her daughter. I have asked the daughter to suck me, too. She now does that too, and I suck her.

Mama has given me a key. Now I come to the house and go to the bedroom, and she is in bed, naked, waiting for me. I went to the bedroom one day, and Mama was there with another woman. They were sucking each other and putting their fingers up each other's asses. They saw me but did not stop what they were doing. I took off my clothes and got in bed between them. I sucked them. They sucked me. I fucked the other woman while sucking Mama. I sucked the other woman and Mama sucked me. I fucked them both in the asses, something I had never done before. While I was fucking one, the other licked my ass and put her fingers in and moved them in and out. That night I came back to the house. I fucked the daughter both in the cunt and in the ass, and we sucked each other.

I have told my wife that many American wives suck their husband's penises. I asked her if she would do that for me. She sucked me and she liked it. She let me suck her and she liked it. I put my penis in her ass. She said it hurt, but she liked it. Her belly is so big that I cannot suck her while she is sucking me. She likes to suck me more than she likes me to suck her. Many times she wakes me in the middle of the night to suck me or have me put my penis up her ass.

I am worried. My wife drinks my sperm several times a day. Will this hurt the baby, and will it do anything to her milk? She has her milk now. Is it all right for me to drink it? Also, I am thinking about not seeing Mama, her friend, and her daughter anymore. This means I will have much more semen for my wife to drink. Will a lot of semen hurt a woman? If this will do her or the baby harm, I will continue with the other three women. I think about them sucking me all the time. I would like to get all three of them in bed together. When I think about my wife and the other women, my penis gets hard and I masturbate.

I saw a beautiful woman on the street the other day. She had the biggest breasts I have ever seen. She saw me looking at them. She told me that for five dollars, I could touch them. I gave her the money. My two hands would not go around one breast. This was very exciting. I went home and my wife sucked me. I wish the girl with the big breasts would let me do more than touch them. Maybe I will meet her again. I am masturbating while I am talking to you. I hope you don't mind.
* * * *

THE PRIEST'S TALE

The author of this little story claims to have been, at one time, a priest. He says his fantasies are recollections of actual events in his life. He uses the fantasies as aids to masturbation and to arouse himself for his sexual partners, male and female. He says he is no longer a Catholic and that he actively despises his former religion, its rituals, practitioners, and the members of its clergy.

* * * * I'm in the rectory, and this pretty little girl and her brand-new husband are in front of me. The husband looks bored to hide his embarrassment at what his bride haltingly tells me. "Father, he . . . um . . . um . . . comes to me with this . . . ah . . . bigness . . . and . . . um . . . he wants to . . . um, ah . . . put it inside my, well between my . . . well, I guess you know what I'm trying to say . . . and I know that if that bigness of his goes where, um, he wants it to go that it will hurt me. He tried to get me to, well, kiss it, or something like that, the very first night, and I almost threw up. I mean that can't be normal. He pushed my head down on it and it almost went . . . well, you can imagine where it almost went . . . and the other thing he wants me to do . . . well, I have to be on my stomach, and the bigness goes, um, in the back, I don't mean in from the back, I mean *in* the back, and I *know* that will hurt. He says all these things he wants to do are all right, but that isn't what the nuns said."

She is squirming with embarrassment, and also she's becoming aroused, remembering his cock. While she speaks, she rubs her thighs and rocks slightly back and forth. I am seated at my desk, which conceals the fact that I have my cock in one hand and a handkerchief in the other.

I launch into the standard lecture on her duties as a wife. I tell her that thus far she has been a bad wife and must mend her ways. The church teaches that any sexual practice that leads to intercourse is not only acceptable, but holy, if done in God's name. If her husband wants to put his penis in her vagina, she must permit him, and it is best if she actually encourages him to do so. Also, he's a fine, athletic-looking young man and he will probably desire intercourse with her many times a day. Each time he wants her, she must joyfully submit to him, unless she is physically ill. Many women prefer not to have intercourse when they are menstruating. If she is such a woman, she has the right to ask him not to approach her at that time. He may accede to her request or he may not. But the choice is his, not hers. If he demands it, she must give it.

I drone on and on. I've given this talk so many times you'd think I'd get bored with it. But it never bores me, it excites me. I see his "bigness" going into her, and my cock, broad and sturdy boyo it is, stands tall and strong.

If her husband wants her to kiss or suck his penis, she must do so. If he desires to ejaculate into her mouth, I suggest she let him. The Church is unclear on this point. Some scholars say she must allow him to ejaculate in her mouth and must swallow his sperm. Others disagree. I myself think she should obey her husband. He loves her, after all, and he will do nothing to her to harm her.

Anal sex is the part of the lecture I like best. I love asshole fucking myself, I love to both give and receive, I tell her that here again, in my opinion, she should obey her husband. I tell her there is nothing frightening or sinful or dirty in anything her young man wants. Moreover, I tell her, she will probably be pleasantly surprised to find she actually enjoys everything he wants of her and will find herself requesting him to make his penis available to her for each of these kinds of intercourse.

Usually, I come about here. The girl stares at me with a combination of disbelief and relief. She's relieved to know she can take the cock anywhere she has secretly wanted it all her life without committing any sin. And, she can't believe that a priest not only knows what her husband wants her to do, he sides with the husband.

The kicker to this little talk of mine is this: I tell them both that I want a telephone call from one of them the following day. I want to hear exactly what he wanted her to do, whether or not she did it, whether she liked it, how many times they did whatever they did, and whether she plans to continue to obey her husband. I beat off to these calls. I always ask the brides if they liked the taste. The honest ones always say yes. God knows they're right.

Another thing I jerk off to is remembering my first fuck. It was with a girl named Sally. We were both twelve. I'd known her all my life. When we were little, we played doctor. We knew each other's bodies in detail, had touched each other in all the interesting places. She put her thumb up my anus when I was about six, and I put a finger in her cunt the same day. Neither she nor I had been as daring with each other since, although she watched, once in a while, while her older brother browned me or had me suck him off. Well, he was too young to be sucked "off." Sucked to "come-less orgasm" is what went on.

We were lying on the grass one evening near her swimming pool. Her parents were in the house. We were lying on our backs, just talking. Between masturbation and sex with her brother, I never thought about girls much. And Sally and I hadn't played doctor or done anything sexual since the day we stuck fingers in each other.

While we were talking, I yawned and stretched and my left hand wound up resting on her belly. Whenever I had touched her before, since we were very little, she had always taken my hand away. I expected her to do so now. But she did not. We continued talking as if nothing had happened. I began caressing her belly and lightly kneading it with my fingers. We had stopped talking, both of us concentrating on what we were feeling. Suddenly, she moved. I thought she would move away, but she didn't. She moved so that my hand now rested on her crotch. It was much warmer than her belly.

I must have let my hand rest there for ten minutes. I was afraid if I moved it, she would move away or take it off. When I finally got enough courage, I pushed on her crotch just a little, and she pushed back. I had her permission, in other words, to do what I was doing. Then I put my hand inside. Her hair was softer than any of the guys I had touched.

I took my hand out of her bathing suit and turned on my side and put my other hand down there. Her eyes were open and she was looking at me, still lying on her back. Then she turned on her side and put her small hand on the front of my trunks where my twelve-year-old cock bulged. She smiled a small smile when she touched me and then reached under the trunks, up through the built-in jock strap, and held my balls and felt my cock. I tried to take the bottom of her bathing suit down and, for a second, she went all stiff. But just for a second. Then she raised up her hips and I slid the bottoms down. She took her hand out of my trunks. I got to my knees, and we both sort of fumbled the trunks off me.

I was now kneeling just a foot or less from her head, and the end of my cock was scant inches from her mouth. She looked at it and she touched it. I wanted her to take it in her mouth, but she didn't. I wanted to put it in her mouth, but I didn't have the nerve. I'd seen lots of boys with penises in their mouths, and I'd had lots of penises in my mouth, but I'd never seen a girl with a penis in her mouth. I wasn't sure girls did such things. To cover my confusion, I suppose, I began kissing her belly, kneeling beside her.

After kissing her a couple of hundred times, I began licking her belly and sucking it and gently biting it, moving my head slowly downward, closer to her hot little cunt.

[Can you imagine an ex-priest writing words like "hot little cunt?"]

I'm erect as I write this.

She moved. She lifted my leg and got her head under me, and we were in the classic sixty-nine position. I didn't know the name of it then, and I had never seen anybody in this position before. My prick was suddenly in her mouth . . . she was sucking on me much harder and better than any boy ever had . . . and my tongue was inside her and outside her and all over and in and around her. This was the best thing that had ever happened to me in my whole life.

Sally and I talked the next day about what we did that evening. We concluded that what we did must have been natural and good because the things we did to each other came to us so spontaneously. I liked what I did to her. I liked the feeling of doing something to her that made her feel good. I told her that I would have liked sucking her pussy even if she were not sucking my cock at the same time. She told me the same thing. And, in the years following, she sucked me off many times while I did nothing to her in return. I did the same for her.

I didn't know anything about girls until this. I didn't know about their wetness and the smell and the taste. Thanks to Sally, I was learning volumes about girls and myself.

As much as I loved eating her, her sucking me was better. That night she had her hands and arms around my ass. She was sort of doing chinning exercises, pulling herself up to get all of me, balls and all, into her mouth and then lowering herself back down so that she was just sucking on the head.

From sucking off boys and being sucked off, I knew that the first time somebody comes in your mouth and really ejaculates, it comes as a surprise. I threw up the first time a boy really shot into my mouth, and I had seen many boys gag, retch, and throw up when others came into their mouths. I felt myself beginning to come. I didn't want to make her throw up, and I tried to move off her. She held my ass tighter so, when I tried to roll off, I wound up on the bottom with her on top, grinding her pussy hard into my face.

I pushed her pussy out of my face so I could breathe. She was pumping her head up and down on my cock, and I was pushing my hips up and down at the same time. I whispered to her to stop. She whispered back that she didn't want to stop. I told her to at least stop for a minute so I could explain something to her. I told her that I was going to come and that the first time somebody comes in your mouth some people get sick. She asked if coming was like piss. I told her no. I explained that it was the color of milk and thick, like hand lotion. She asked what it would taste like. I told her it didn't taste like anything else but itself, but it was good.

I liked talking to her pussy like this, and I could feel her breath on my cock when she whispered back. She wanted to know why, if it tasted good, people got sick. I said because it squirts into your mouth and up against the back of your throat and it's a little like putting your finger down your throat.

Her hair was brushing against my legs, balls, and cock. It was a reflex action on my part, not consciously planned, but my pelvis, automatically and on its own, rolled up and I was in her mouth again. She wanted me in her mouth as much and as automatically and naturally as I wanted to be there. She began sucking harder than before. I could feel her lips in my hair and her nose on my balls. I went back to sucking her and tried to suck her as hard as she was sucking me. I pulled her down on me as hard as I could and licked her ass. That really got her excited. I put a finger up there as far as I could and moved it in and out and sucked her cunt at the same time. She was really wriggling. When I came, she gagged and took her mouth off me to get her breath for a second. Then she dove back down on it and finished me off. She rolled off me and lay on her back on the grass with her legs apart, panting. I rolled over and sucked her once or twice and started kissing her higher and higher. She had come on her mouth and chin. I licked it off while getting myself in position to get my cock in her.

She was wet and ready for me. I jammed into her hard, just as if I were fucking one of my friends. She gasped and jumped and lost her virginity. She went limp for a couple of seconds, and I continued pumping in and out of her fast and furiously. I came again and fell on top of her, exhausted.

We did this, with variations, almost every day for years.

Sister Helena came to the convent next door the last year of my priesthood. She impressed everyone favorably. She was popular with her students and the entire staff, including and especially me. I must have looked horny the day she was ushered into my study to be introduced. I stood up and shook her hand. She blushed and cast her eyes down. My cock stirred. I masturbated after she left.

She selected me as her regular confessor, and she used the confessional to let me know that I could fuck her if I wished. I used to masturbate while she confessed her sinful thoughts and activities. She was a masturbator, she said, and she masturbated while she thought about me and the goodies concealed beneath my cassock. "I know it's a sin, Father," she used to say, "but I think about you and your penis. I wonder if you ever get erections, if you've ever had a woman, if you ever think about me like this. I can't seem to help myself. When I think about you, I masturbate. Sometimes I think about you masturbating. I used to watch my brother do it. I loved to see the sperm shooting out of him."

On and on she rambled like this, week after week. How I managed not to fuck that woman for so long, I'll never know. Well, I suppose I do know: I was getting into one of the widows in the parish, I was masturbating every day, and the gardener and I had a thing going.

After Helena had been with us for about a year, I finally broke down. I came home from the widow late one night and saw that Helena's light was still on. I used my key to let myself in the front door of the convent. I went to her room, very quietly turned the knob on the door, and slipped in without knocking.

She was lying across the bed with her knees up, her legs spread, and her head hanging down over the side, so she could not see me. She was masturbating with the base of the crucifix that was supposed to be hanging on the wall. I very quietly undressed, leaving my shoes and clothes in a heap where I stood. I went over to her and knelt by her head. Her eyes were shut and she still did not know I was in the room. I whispered her name softly and she opened her eyes. For a moment, she went rigid with terror. Upside down she didn't recognize me for a brief instant. I suppose she thought I was a rapist. When she finally recognized me, she smiled and said, "Well, it certainly took you long enough to get here, Joe." She pulled my cock into her mouth, still upside down, and continued masturbating. What a fine night this turned out to be. The widow and I had made love about an hour earlier. It took a long time for me to come the first time with Helena. That suited her fine. She loved sucking cock, she told me, the longer the better. After I came in her mouth, I rested for a few minutes. She continued to masturbate. When I was rested, and my cock was standing up again, I rolled her over on her side and rimmed her while she moved the crucifix in and out of herself. I put my cock up against her asshole, tentatively. She reached a hand back and guided me inside her. It was exciting fucking her like this because not only did plunging in and out of her feel marvelous, I could feel the cross moving in and out of her, which made it even better. After I came, I went to sleep still inside her. She woke me hours later. The lights were out and the first light of dawn was beginning to show. I immediately got a hard on, and we made love. We had to do it on the floor because her cot squeaked.

She came to the rectory twice the next day and blew me each time and made me promise to come to her that night. For the entire time she was with us, I went to her every night. I gave up the gardener and the widow. * * * *

I suppose many readers will find this upsetting, particularly Roman Catholics who are of the opinion that nuns and priests don't do things like this. I hope they find consolation in the fact that the man who sent this in claimed to be a priest, but offered no evidence for it except a level of literacy suggesting the amount of education a priest might be expected to have. Or, that anybody with a college degree, priest or not, might have. I have shown his typewritten letter to a number of Catholic friends. They tell me that, since he makes no errors, he is probably not what he claims. The lecture he gave the bride follows the Catholic line, but it is more explicit than such lectures usually are. The consensus of my Catholic friends is that the letter was probably the handiwork of an intelligent, depraved Catholic (of the fallen-away variety, of course) layman.

LIBERTY LOVER

The man who wrote me the following fantasy called me on the phone after I had received his letter to ask if I would use it in the book. I told him I thought it was a nice little story and I would use it. The man became highly indignant and said what he had written me was not a "story" but literal truth. I like this one better than any other in the book, with the possible exception of the one on page 116, about a man from another planet.

* * * * Every night, when nobody is looking, I swim out to

Bedloe's Island and meet my lover. The island is closed to the public at night and she gets very lonely. She is always glad to see me. She lays down her torch and gathers me into her arms and hugs and kisses me. She's French, you know, and loves to suck cock. She blows me a couple of times and after that, I take off her lovely green gown and just ball the ass off her. A couple of nights ago we both got so tired that we went to sleep in each other's arms. We awakened after dawn and were terrified that someone had noticed that she was not standing up and holding her torch like always and also that she had no clothes on. She got dressed in a hurry and picked up the torch. I kept a close eye on the papers for a couple of days. We were lucky. Nobody saw us. * * * *

MASSEUSE

* * * * When my wife and I got married, nobody could have been straighter than the two of us. Straight missionary-position sex. *Playboy,* let's hear it for good old *Playboy,* changed all that. I bought my first copy, and she and I started reading it in bed. We started learning things like a blow job is done by nice girls too; pussy tastes great; the asshole has other uses than we had supposed; sex with other couples is fun; sexual aids, like dildos and vibrators, make the experience much more intense than we had believed possible; sex with huge groups of strangers is warm and human; and watching one spouse having sex with maybe thirty people over a weekend is marvelous.

When we first got married, she didn't work. I was a freelance photographer making about $1,500 a month. We lived on it just fine. But, when we started doing group sex, our expenses went up and my income went down because I no longer worked on weekends. Weekends, we flew all over the country and Canada for the mass gangbangs. She had to go to work. She wasn't experienced at anything.

She asked me one day what I thought about her going to work in a massage parlor, doing for pay during the week what we spent money for on the weekends. At first I was really turned off. She would be balling guys and I couldn't watch.

Well, this big Canadian weekend came up, and we didn't want to miss it. More than a thousand couples were going. But we couldn't afford to go. So I told her to try to get a job in a massage parlor for a week, just long enough to raise enough money so we could get to the Canadian bash.

I'll tell you, the first day she went to work, I was nervous as hell and so was she. But, by the end of the week, after she had made more than $1,100 and looked on the whole experience as just a job, I was considerably calmed. Calm enough to suggest that she continue the job when we got back from the weekend.

Sometimes she makes as much as $500 a night. When she gets home at three or four in the morning, she's really bushed. She gets in the tub and I give her a bath and then we have supper together and she tells me about her day. All of it, every detail. By the time she's through, we're both horny as minks. We go to bed and ball till we're exhausted.

The massage parlor is a negotiated thing. The idea is for the girl to get as much money as she possibly can from the customer. The ideal is to get it all. And it's relatively simple to do. You can tell a $50 suit from a $300 job without much trouble. And shoes are a good indicator of wealth. So what my wife does is first size the customer up. If he's rich, he'll pay her $75 or $100 for a blow job. If he's not so rich, he gets the same thing for $20 or $25.

The statistics in her work run like this (in case you care): 50 percent blow jobs, 25 percent hand jobs, 25 percent fucking.

Her customers are all kinds of people. She has a set of regulars. One is a tubby little man named Rabbit. Rabbit likes her to hit him and spank him with a hairbrush. He likes her to spank him with the bristle side till he bleeds. He likes it when she shouts dirty names at him. She once told him to play dog for her. She'd throw her slipper across the room and he'd have to fetch it back for her in his mouth. Rabbit's greatest kick is when she knocks him down and orders him to lick her cunt. She says, for a little, tubby man, he sure is good at this. He's one of the few customers who brings her off.

It's funny. Rabbit does all the work and she gets paid for it.

There's an Englishman who comes to her once a week. For $100, all she has to do is watch him put the hairbrush handle up his ass and move it in and out a few times till he comes. She has offered to do this for him, but he says no, he'd rather do it himself.

A lot of the men who come in are nervous and afraid to tell her what they want. She's really great at relaxing them and has a set little routine she uses on them. She lays them on the table and pours oil on their backs and begins the massage. She spends a lot of time around the ass, kneading their cheeks and getting as close to their assholes as she can without touching. Then she rolls them over and puts on more oil. She starts at their feet and begins moving upward. When she gets a little above the knees, she starts her routine. It really turns me on when she does the routine for me. "Do you mind if I talk to you a little bit while I work?" she asks. The nervous ones have been hoping she'd say something to break the ice, and they always say something like, "Yes, please do talk. I'm sure it will relax me."

"Well," she begins, "I'm sure you're here just for a massage. No funny business or anything like that and that's why the manager sent you to me. I'm the only girl here who gives just massage. I've been here for a year and I've never done, well, you know, anything immodest. I'm a happily married woman and wouldn't dream of cheating on my husband.

"Until now.

"I have never in my life seen a penis as beautiful as yours. It's all I can do to keep my hands off it. It's so big and hairy and mean-looking, and it would feel so good inside of me, anyplace inside of me. I'm sure you're married and faithful to your wife, but this is almost more than I can stand. Can I suck it? I think, if I can't have it in my mouth just for a taste, I'll just die. If you let me suck it, it's not really cheating. It's not as if we're having real intercourse, is it?"

Well, by this time, if he's a normal guy, his cock is throbbing and if she doesn't start sucking on it soon, *he's* the one who's going to die.

The guy says go ahead and suck it, or he tells her whatever else it is he wants and she starts and then stops. She goes into the last part of the bit. "The other girls all charge for doing what I'm doing because I couldn't help myself. I think they charge (and she names whatever figure she thinks she can get away with at this point) for doing it.

Would you object to paying me that much? I'll put the money in the kitty secretly so that no one will know I've fallen just this once. I think it would be unfair to the other girls if we did not contribute."

The guy always says yes, he'll pay whatever she asks. His ego is so puffed up, he'd pay anything. And also the "if we did not contribute" line is the real kicker. They're in a conspiracy together, and he's not buying the services of a whore, he's making a contribution, for God's sake, like to a church or something.

This routine of hers works so well that a lot of these guys become regular customers. When they come back a second time, she pretends to get all carried away the moment they show up. If there are other girls around in the reception room when he gets out of the elevator, she goes up to him possessively and takes his arm and says "This man is mine. He's here for a massage only. Isn't that so, darling?" Well, this really makes him feel swell. When they get inside and she tears her clothes off and instantly starts blowing him or whatever it is he wants, it's really great for the guy. And he comes fast, so it's less work for her.

A couple of these guys have told her they love her and that they will "take her away from all this." She tells them she loves them with every fibre of her being, but she is the sole support of a crippled husband who needs constant attention if he is to survive. She makes a reference to what the nurse charges her to care for her husband while she's working and the high costs of doctors and medicines. Most of the time this runs her price up.

She's probably making more money than anybody in the joint.

One of her repeats is a guy who takes his clothes off, undresses her, then takes hold of his cock and jerks off while she dances around him. When he's shot his wad, he thanks her and gives her $100 and leaves. He's in and out of the room in less than ten minutes, and she doesn't even have to touch him. Nice work for $100.

She had a fella come in the other day who paid $75 for the privilege of putting his finger in her ass while he jerked off. One guy pours wine in her cunt and sucks it out. I forget what he pays. Another guy rubs his cock on her tits till he comes. Other guys like to come on her and lick it off. One of these is a man who likes her to suck him off and then

French-kiss him and give him his come back in his mouth. And, believe it or not, there are guys who really don't want anything but a massage. She goes through that little routine of hers I told you about, and they turn her down.

She's been getting very much into the bisexual scene now. There's a girl there she's been balling for months when business is slow. She's brought her home a number of times and we do threesomes. We kind of think of her as a toy. The chick really turns on when I take the top and my wife takes the bottom or vice versa, or when I take the front and my wife gets the back. She just loves all the attention we give her. She's a freaky chick. She likes to lie on the bed with one dildo up her cunt, one up her ass, and one in her mouth, watching my wife and me ball. Then she likes my wife to do the same thing while we ball. And she likes me to do somewhat the same thing while she and my wife ball. She likes me to have one up my ass and one in my mouth while I work on her ass with the third. She really likes me to whang the hell out of that ass of hers. When she starts saying, "Now, now, now, now, now," it's her signal to me that she's coming, she wants the dildo out and me in. If I can come fast enough so she can come with me, she says that's best for her.
* * * *

This man rambled on for hours. You'll note that he mentions having been a photographer and the subject never comes up again. I gather that now he has no employment save fixing his wife's breakfast and dinner and probably keeping their dwelling cleaned and dusted. And, of course, screwing. He is, in short, a housewife, the most boring and stultifying occupation yet invented, next to being vice president of the United States.

FIVE GRAND A WEEK

This man is a reasonably well-known New York mobster. That's all I can tell you.
* * * * The papers say I'm a mobster. They're wrong. I don't belong to a mob and I don't have a mob of people working for me. I

own a number of businesses, all illegal. I suppose I'm what could be called a racketeer. I think of myself as a crook and I enjoy being a crook. I do less work than other businessmen and make a helluva lot more money than they do. Which is only fair. My risks are greater. I can get killed doing what I do, or I can be jailed if I get caught.

I make about five grand a week. That's not much, but it's enough so that I can do pretty much what I want. The things I want sexually would scare the shit out of my wife, so I do the massage-parlor thing. I go to Caesar's, the best and most expensive parlor in the city. When I get there, I have a plan. I know exactly what I'm going to have done to me because I've planned it all in advance. The planning is what you want to hear from me, but you can figure what I fantasize about has happened.

I go in and pay the fee and go off and take a shower. Sometimes I pick just one girl, sometimes two, sometimes three. However many girls I pick, they each get $500, and it is understood that for that kind of money, anything goes. Anything I want, they do, no questions asked; they can't deny me anything.

I like every kind of sex a man can have with a woman. I like to spank a little bit and I like to be spanked a little. Spanking three women at once is a great thrill. Spanking two women while a third spanks me is also fun.

I like asses. I screw one girl in the ass while another is working on me with a dildo and I'm licking off another. Sometimes one girl rims me and I rim another and the third blows me. Some days I go in and get three blow jobs, one right after the other. And they have to swallow it. Most whores don't swallow it. They give so many blow jobs during the course of a day, it would make them sick if they did. For my kind of money, they make an exception. The third girl really has to earn her money. I once went for forty-five minutes before I came. Damn near wore her out. She was all sweaty, she was working so hard. I felt sorry for her after a while and asked her if she wanted one of the other girls to take over. She shook her head no, and when she was through, she said she kind of liked the challenge of the thing. Whores always put the johns on, but I thought that was a pretty good crack.

One of the more exciting things I do is sixty-nine one girl while another works on her with a dildo and the other is ramming one up my ass. Whores seldom come in their work. They save it for their husbands and boyfriends, but this particular trick really turns them on.

Right after World War II, I was stationed in Japan and got a basket fuck. It was so good, I used to spend most of my pay on them. The girl gets into a basket suspended from the ceiling. I'd lay on the floor and she lowers the basket down on my cock until it's inside her. Then she makes the basket spin. This is best for ass-fucking because asses are so much tighter. I always wanted a blow job like this, but none of the girls could get into the right position for it. I ate a girl in the basket once. It was great for both of us. I got permission from the owner once to bring my own girl, the one I was living with. I got her in the basket and ate her. She started screaming it felt so good. I thought she didn't like it so I stopped. Then she started screaming again because I'd stopped. I don't know how many times she came, but my face was sure covered with pussy juice.

Sometimes, with the girls, we play switch. One girl shoves the dildo or vibrator up in me and the two other girls bend over. I shove my cock in the first girl just once. Then I take it out and put it in the other girl just once and then return to the first girl. I really like this a lot because I last so long before I come. If you think about it, you'll see why. The amount of time you spend moving from girl to girl is long, so it slows you down.

I go in for water sports there. Pee is a turn on for me. Sometimes when I'm alone, I'll pee down my leg and think one of the whores is doing it to me. That really gets my cock up in a hurry.

The reason I go to Caesar's so much is my wife. She's Italian and goes to mass every day of her life. If I try to have sex with her more than a couple of times a month, she starts looking at me like I'm some kind of sex maniac. She was raised to think sex is dirty. You can blame the damned church for that.

At times I play a kind of game at Caesar's. One girl gives me a hand job and another one kneels six or eight inches away and tries to catch the come in her mouth. They have and use Polaroid cameras there. I have a photograph of this in my wallet. You can see the stuff shooting out and everything.

I have an electric scalp massager at home. I use it on myself once in a while. I can make myself come fast when I use it on my cock, or slow if I put it on my ass. Got drunk one night and touched my wife's cunt with it. Christ, she yelled at me for an hour. * * * *

MY WIFE SHOWS HERSELF

* * * * My wife is a real knockout and she knows it. She knows that my friends like to look at her breasts. So she wears bikinis and low-cut dresses. When my friends look at her and want her, it really turns me on. We've never spoken about it, but I'm sure she knows. She was being fitted for some shoes the other day. She spread her legs just enough so the clerk could get a good look, but not enough so that it was obvious. She gave me a sly look to make sure I knew what she was doing. I rarely masturbate, but when we got home that day I did. While I was doing it, I was thinking about that clerk and what he saw up her dress.

Sometimes, when we're making love, I see her balling or sucking my friends.

I have one long fantasy that I return to often. It's pure fantasy. I want a picture of my wife for my office desk. We go to a photographer. She goes into his studio and I wait outside in the anteroom. She doesn't know it, but I can see into the studio without being seen. I watch to see if she's going to spread her legs a little to give him a look, or expose a little more breast than necessary.

The photographer is a young guy. He seats her on a couch in front of his big portrait camera. He arranges her this way and that trying to find a pose he likes. While he's doing it, he's looking down the front of her dress. He gets an erection. Seeing him, I do too. My wife looks at it. It frightens her. She just likes to turn men on in front of me and I'm not there. I make a small movement of some kind so she can see me. Our eyes meet and I give her a little nod, letting her know everything is okay.

Well, in real life, as I say, she just turns my friends on a little bit, but this is fantasy.

I'm terribly embarrassed telling you this. Do you find what I'm telling you repellent or do you want me to go on?

She looks at the erection through his pants. He sees her looking. He puts her hand on it. I expect her to be shocked and take her hand away. But she doesn't. She strokes him. He asks her if she'd like to see it. She nods enthusiastically. She looks at me to make sure I'm watching. Not only am I watching, I have taken my penis out and I'm playing with it. The photographer takes his out. He's fully erect. As I say, she's sitting down and he's standing over her. I suppose you can imagine what happens next. Well, maybe you can't. He doesn't ask her to do it, she asks him if he'll let her. Then she does it, but she doesn't do it the way she does with me. With me, she sucks me, it's sort of quiet and tender and one of a thousand things she does for me to tell me "I love you." But with the photographer it's an entirely animal thing. She makes loud slurping noises. The photographer has her by the ears and he's thrusting into her and I'm sure she's being hurt. I start to go to her aid. She sees me and waves me away.

The photographer is so violent, I don't see how she can stand it. He's really ramming into her hard. I wonder how much longer he can go before he has an orgasm. He finally has it. I can tell because I see his semen running down her chin. Now at last he'll stop, I think to myself. But he doesn't. Instead, he climbs on top of her, still in her mouth, laying her down on the sofa on her back and continues even more frenetically than before. His sperm runs down her cheeks. I don't know if he has come again or if it's left over from the first time.

One of her arms is hanging down. She beckons me with her hand to come into the room. She raises her rear up, indicating that she wants me inside her. I get inside her, very gently, so as not to let the photographer know I'm there. He's so carried away by what he's doing that he does not notice me. Watching her and the photographer, I know now that she likes roughness in sex. I flail away at her in a way I never do in real life. I fuck her like the men in porno films fuck the women. I'm really brutal. She responds with orgasm after orgasm. She squeezes me with her vagina, something she does in real life, and I respond with a fine orgasm that just goes on and on. I leave her and go back to the anteroom. In a little while, she comes out looking as if nothing had happened.

I wonder how she'd react if I told her this. Do other men have fantasies as vivid as this?

I fantasize often about taking our picture during sex with a Polaroid camera. One of my friends has an attaché case full of photographs of him and his wife and other women. He shows them to me, and it's embarrassing. I know his wife and some of the other women. He says the presence of a camera makes sex much more intense because both partners tend to perform. He said he had been trying to have sex from the back, anal sex, with his wife for years, but she always refused. The first night he used the Polaroid, she let him in. He says the pictures are useful in other ways, too. When he tells women about them, women he has not had sex with, they always ask to see. When they run across pictures of women they know, they invariably get aroused, much to his advantage. I fantasize once in a while that I'm going through his pictures and I come across one of my wife. I take it home and show it to her, and she tells me she let him take it knowing that I would see it. * * * *

I LIKE OTHER MEN TO SEE HER

* * * * When my wife and I make love, I imagine that other men are watching. I see her standing naked in front of a window with the shade up. She is masturbating. The people across the street can see her. I saw a dildo in a sex shop in Japan. It was a huge rubber thing about eighteen inches long and as thick as my wrist. I didn't buy it, but I picture my wife standing in front of the window sucking on it and

putting it up her cunt. She puts it up inside her ass and blows me with all the lights on and the shades up. I wish I'd bought that dildo. I've been trying to talk her into buying a vibrator. I have told her exactly what I'd like her to do with it. She goes over to the window and puts her foot on the sill. She rubs her cunt and asshole with it. She puts it inside herself while I watch her and masturbate.

We throw a party for our friends. I stand on a chair in the middle of the room. She takes my cock out and sucks me off in front of everybody. She's working on herself with the dildo while she sucks. I squeeze her shoulder, our signal that I am about to come. She gives me one final deep suck and takes her mouth away so everybody can see how much come I am able to give her. In the fantasy I come much more than in real life. The juice is really coming out hard. Great big spurts of it that she catches in her mouth. As the spurts get smaller and smaller, her mouth comes in closer and closer, and at the end I'm back in her mouth again. She is so good at it that my knees get weak. Our friends break into applause. "Encore, encore," they yell.

She does it all over again.

She lies on her back on the bed. Her legs are spread wide apart. Her cunt is wet and open. It's red and beautiful. The lights are on and the shades are up. She's masturbating slowly with the fingers of one hand while she holds herself open with the fingers of the other. I'm standing over her masturbating. When I come, I come on her breasts. We both like to do this in real life. We both think about it a lot. Sometimes, we describe what the two of us are doing to each other. Then we both get very aroused and either do it or have sex in some other way.

Sometimes instead of asking her to masturbate for me, I ask her to roll over on her stomach and get on all fours. We have one of those four-battery flashlights. It comes to a blunt, round end. She puts Vaseline on the flashlight and on and in her ass. She puts it in herself all the way up to the switch, about eight or nine inches. She puts it in slowly and moves it in and out of herself slowly. With her other hand, she masturbates herself. Sometimes we vary this. Sometimes I sit on the bed crosslegged and she goes down on me while the flashlight goes in and out and she massages her clitoris. Her dressing table is between the windows at the foot of the bed. I can see what she's doing in the mirror. While she's blowing me, I tell her what I can see. It really excites her when I talk. She says the position is uncomfortable as hell and going down on me like this makes her feel as if she is going to smother. She says the discomfort and the smothering feeling add to her pleasure. Every now and then we talk about doing this in front of our friends in real life.

My wife is here beside me listening to me talk to you. I just touched her cunt. She's all excited listening to what I'm saying and so am I. She's masturbating herself and sucking me as we talk. God, what a great cocksucker she is.

A fantasy we both enjoy is talking about my friends fucking her while I watch, and her watching me ball her girlfriends. She's seen a number of her friends with no clothes on and she describes them for me. She tells me about how much hair they have, what color it is, how big their tits are, what the nipples are like. She and her girlfriends talk about their sex lives just like men do. They tell each other what they like best, who has what kind of cock, which guy likes to do what in bed.

It never fails to amaze me how you can't tell what a girl likes in bed from looking at her or talking with her. Some of her girlfriends look like real sex machines and their sex lives consist of getting laid once in a while in the missionary position. They wouldn't dream of sucking a cock or letting anybody do anything to their assholes. And her quiet, shy, mousey girlfriends turn out to be the real cockhounds.

No, she's never had sex with a girl. But if we ever get enough courage to have sex with our friends, she's going to. She says the thought of having sex with another girl sort of turns her off. But she knows what a kick I'm going to get out of watching her, so she'll do it to please me. Also, she says she knows she's going to hate watching me do to another girl what the two of us do together. What she hates most about the whole thing is that she knows I'm going to be enjoying myself. I keep telling her that while I'm balling some other girl, I'll be looking at her and pretending that what I'm doing, I'm doing with her. Also there's no love involved. I love her and her only. She puts her foot down on letting other people use the flashlight. She says it's a very special instrument and it's just for us. If I want her to use the light in front of our friends, she'll do it. But she won't let anybody else but me touch it.

She's finger-fucking herself now with both hands. One hand is working on her cunt, and she has two fingers up her ass while she's blowing me. It's exciting to watch. You know, if she enjoys the discomfort of the position and the feeling of being smothered, maybe she'd enjoy the S and M scene. I've never tried it, and we've never talked about it. Let me try some S and M talk now, okay, honey? She nodded yes.

If you don't suck harder, I'm going to spank you. I'm going to tie you to the radiator over there and stick that Japanese dildo I told you about up your ass. I'm going to stick another one up your cunt and make you sit down so they go all the way up inside you. I'm going to put another one in your mouth. I'll put a string around the one in your mouth so you can't spit it out. I'm going to ram it all the way down your throat. It'll be just like my cock when it goes down except it's much thicker than me and much longer. When you're all trussed up like that, I'm going to turn out all the lights and leave the room and shut the door. You won't know whether I'm in the room or not. Oh yes, you'll have a blindfold on, and rubber plugs in your ears. The only way you'll know whether I'm with you or not is if I sneak up on you and slap you or push that dildo down your throat a little farther. Is this turning you on? Do you like what I'm saying to you? How about that? She does. How about you, Mr. Price, [Price was the false name I used in the newspaper advertising. W.J.S.] are you grooving on this shit? Does it turn you on?

You know what I'm doing is manufacturing fantasies for you right on the spot. These are brand new fantasies I've never had before. Excuse me while I come. . . . Are you really, no shit, writing a book? Or do you just like to listen to people talk sex to you over the phone? I must say I read a lot and I never heard of a writer named Bill Price. You're in the current issue of *Argosy,* are you? Well, how am I supposed to know which article is yours if you won't tell me your name?

Did you read *The Story of O?* Remember those peg boards? Well, in the book there are these peg boards the women are forced to sit on to keep their assholes nice and loose for the men who own the women. I'll bet I could rig up something with the flashlight so that Nancy could sit on it. I think it'd be nice to come home from work one day and find her sitting on it for me. I think if I came into the bedroom after work, and there she was sitting on it for me, I'd get so excited, I'd come in my pants. If it weren't for that switch, I'll bet she could sit on it right down to the floor.

Did I tell you about my cock? Well, it's bigger than most. She says it's the biggest one she ever saw. Sometimes when I'm fucking her, it hurts her it goes in so deep. Sometimes I slam into some kind of wall in there and it hurts *me.* But there's no end to this ass of hers. The deeper the cock goes in, the better it is for both of us. And if it weren't for the switch, I'll just bet she could take the whole thing up there. The switch on the flashlight, I mean.

I've got to think of something shaped like that, that doesn't have a switch on it. Damn, I wish I had bought that dildo. A cucumber, maybe? Thick enough but too short. A vibrator's too short, too. I've seen some wine bottles that might do the trick. You know the long skinny ones at the top that go down to a thick base? I wonder if her asshole can stretch enough to take it at the base. Wine bottle is no good, come to think of it, it's glass. It might break inside her and hurt her. Kill her, even.

I've got it. I saw some dowels in the hardware store the other day. They're thicker than a cock, but not so much thicker that it would hurt her. I'll buy one of those things, saw it off at about two feet, round off the end, sandpaper it till it's smooth as glass, and put about ten coats of shellac on it. Perfect. I wonder how deep she'll be able to get it in?

I've heard of dildos that squirt warm come-like stuff into women. The girl squeezes it when she has an orgasm and it feels like a man coming inside her. Maybe the simplest thing to do would be to go to a sex shop and just buy the stuff we want. I know I'll never have the nerve to go in a place like that. Maybe Nancy does. * * * *

In the course of researching the book it developed that this particular fantasy, having sexual relations in front of friends and strangers, is among the commonest. I collected possibly thirty such fantasies, this one being the most complex and detailed. About half the men reporting claim to have acted this behavior out in real life.

SPECIAL DELIVERY

I have known a number of postmen in my time. Most of them look like railway conductors, and railway conductors, as Russell Baker and other sages have noted, tend to look like bank presidents. And, like bank presidents, they seem a little dull. Postmen, I mean.

This man is a postman I met in a bar. He is not dull.

* * * * There is a woman on my route that I have wanted to fuck for years. You know how some women just plain turn you on? Well, this one does it for me. When I'm banging my wife, I think of her. Sometimes thinking about her gets me so worked up, I think about jacking off, something I have not done since I got married.

She's a redhead. A real one, with the milky white skin that goes along with it. Big tits. *Playboy*-quality tits. Unbelievably fine. Tall and slender with a nice round ass. The ass is big. When I deliver packages to her—two or three times a year—it's all I can do to keep my hands off her. Several times, I've delivered packages there and she's been in a bathrobe. I know she's naked under it.

I gave her the look once. The "I want to fuck you" look. She saw it and smiled. But it wasn't a "come hither" smile. It was just a nice, frank smile that said: "It's nice you want to fuck me. I'm flattered, but I'm fucking somebody else and I'm faithful to him. Maybe some other time."

What I'm telling you is real life. Here's the fantasy:

I am a kid, and I belong to a gang. It is a sex gang. All the guys are fucking and sucking all the other guys. All the girls are treated as common property.

When I first start hanging out with these guys, I never join in. If someone wants to blow me, I say no. If they insist, I tell them I have syph or the clap or crabs or something and get out of it that way. The only thing I'm good for is blow jobs, and I don't like blowing guys and do it as few times as I can without being a shit about it.

I go to sleep in the clubhouse one day. I wake up and the entire bunch is standing over me. The leader tells me that that is my day to be initiated. That means that I have to take my clothes off and let everybody stand around me in a circle and jerk off on me. I tell him I do not want to join. They tear my clothes off and learn my terrible secret.

They find that my cock, when erect, is less than two inches long. They laugh and laugh at my tiny cock. They punch a hole in the foreskin and put a tiny antique lock through the hole. The lock is attached to a chain and the chain goes around my waist. They retain the key. They tell me if I ever find a girl who would like to fuck me after she has seen my cock, I'm to come back and tell the gang. They will unlock me and come with me and watch me fuck her. We will have a gangbang and everybody will fuck her.

One day I come up with this neat plan to get into the readhead's pants. I buy a vibrator, load it with batteries, and mail it to her. The package comes into the station, I put it in my bag and make all my drops and save her for last. I ring the doorbell and there is no answer. I notice that the door is open, which is not safe in this city, and I call out to her to come and shut it. No answer. Maybe there's been trouble, I think. So I go into the house for a look. There she is, lying on a sofa sleeping. She's in her robe. I can see the red hair between her legs, and one of her tits has fallen out.

I go over to the sofa and stand by her. I get a hard on just looking. I touch her nipple and she wakes up. She looks at me and the bulge in my pants and she says, "Hello, Michael."

I ask her how she knows my name, and she says she has known my name for years but doesn't know how. She sees that her crotch and one tit are exposed. She covers herself and leaves the room. She comes back in a minute, dressed in a see-through thing. My bulge increases.

I hand her the package. She opens it and takes out the vibrator. She touches the front of my pants. She asks me if I am as big as the vibrator. I lie and tell her yes. She asks me to show her, a moment I have dreaded all my life. I stall. I ask to see hers. She raises her gown, or whatever it is, and there it is. I get down on my knees in front of her and start licking. She likes it, but she tells me she wants to do sixty-nine. She starts undoing my pants. I'm in a panic. She sees my cock and she tells me it's the loveliest little thing she has ever seen. She says she's wanted to suck one like that all her life. "Take the lock off," she says, "so I can give it a suck without breaking my teeth."

She licks the head of it and it's so good that I come. It excites her, my coming, and she jams the vibrator inside herself. Ten inches long it is, and three inches across. She takes it all and turns it on.

She falls on the floor and writhes in ecstasy. I tell her about my agreement with the gang. She says if it takes a gangbang to get my cock in her mouth, she'll go for a gangbang. I run and get the boys. They unlock me, and we all go back. She is still on the floor when we get there. It's like the other guys aren't there. She takes out the vibrator, never taking her eyes off this tiny prick of mine, and all the guys fuck her, front and back, while she jerks off two others at a time. But she doesn't suck anybody but me. She doesn't even look at anybody but me. After everybody has fucked her and been jerked off a few times, they put on their clothes and leave. She tells me she's rich. I can quit my job and she will spend the rest of her life sucking me off and using the vibrator on herself and letting me lick her beautiful red-haired cunt.

* * * *

IMPROVING REALITY

A writer of the dashing variety—he is forever whipping off to foreign lands to live among head hunters, parachuting into volcanoes, and performing all manner of derring-do in the pursuit of material for books and magazine articles—tells me he has two fantasies, both based on real-life activities, and he insists that both fantasies are much better than the reality.

* * * * The boat lets me off near the South African coast. I get out and begin walking to shore. The shoreline is peopled by dozens of little black girls, all of them ten or eleven years old. They have never seen a white man before, particularly a six-foot-four white man with a blazing red beard and dark glasses. The girls are intrigued by what they see splashing through the water toward them. They dash out to greet me. They climb all over me. Some kiss me, some pull at my hair. Others rub my skin to see if my white color is some kind of dye. With all these pretty little girls crawling around me and touching me everywhere, I become aroused. The girls see my pants bulging and they get excited, too. Right there in the water, we begin having a terrific orgy. The air is warm and the water is cool; I am white and huge and they are black and small. The contrasts are wonderful and we all have a wonderful time.
* * * *

The reality is nowhere near as good, the writer informs me. Actually the little girls came out to greet him. And they did crawl all over him and pull his beard and try to rub the whiteness off his skin. But that was all.

The other fantasy I have is also much better than the reality.

* * * * I go into a bar. Two of my old girl friends are there. We have some drinks and all three of us start feeling kind of horny. We go to one of the girl's apartments and spend the rest of the night doing everything to each other it's physically possible for three human beings to do. I mean we do *everything!* Along about dawn the girls fall asleep. I put my clothes on and go home. * * * *

The reality the fantasy is based on is exactly as he reported it. But the fantasy is much more fun. "In the first place," he says, "screwing with two people is distracting. When I'm eating a girl, I like her to think about me and what I'm doing and not the girl she is eating at the same time. And when a girl is sucking me off, I like to watch her and feel all the marvelous things she's doing with her mouth and my cock. It's just plain distracting to have another girl thrusting her cunt in your face while that's going on. The fantasy also leaves out how tired fucking two women at once becomes. I mean I can have two or three orgasms of an evening and wake up feeling great the next day. But ten orgasms is a real wipeout. After I got my clothes on, it was all I could do to walk home. I felt a hundred and eight years old.

"Also my cock was all swollen and red and sore. Before I went to bed, I ran cold water on the poor thing to get the swelling down."

TEENY BOPPER

Toward the end of researching this book, I rented an automatic telephone answering device so that people could phone in their fantasies whether I was in the office or not. This fantasy comes from a man who describes himself as forty-seven years old, a college graduate, married, and heterosexual.

* * * * I am on a beach in the Caribbean. Naked. A group of teenage girls approaches me. They stand around me in a circle looking down at me. I am lying on my back. For some reason I cannot move. One of the girls kneels down beside me. My penis is soft. She puts it between her breasts and moves herself slowly up and down. My penis becomes erect. She rubs the head of it against her nipples. I come. The white stuff splashes all over her nipples. It drips down onto her belly. She rubs her hands in the white stuff. Then she licks her hand. She tells me it tastes good. One by one, every girl in the group does this to me. As I'm telling you this, I am masturbating. * * * *

ANTHROPOLOGY

* * * * My wife and I have everything in common except sex and location. We both got our undergraduate and graduate degrees from the same universities and we are both anthropologists engaged in field work. We are together one month a year, during our vacations. The rest of the time, we are on separate continents. Because of the nature of our work, the study of extant primitive people, our knowledge of the sexual practices and habits of humans is extensive, and our frankness in discussing sexuality, our own and those of the cultures we observe, is complete. My wife sleeps with other men. I know this because she tells me in her letters about the men (and women) she has sex with. I sleep with other women and write her about it.

This arrangement probably seems odd to you and possibly immoral. But to us, it seems neither. My wife and I love each other and recognize each other's sexual needs. To remain celibate for eleven months at a stretch is unrealistic, or it is for us, and it gives us both pleasure to know that each of us is enjoying all aspects of life, including sex, to the fullest.

Mary (not her real name) and I write each other almost every day, and we mail what we have written to each other about once a month. Once a month, then, we get nice thick letters. In the letters, we talk about our work and our lives. The reason you are reading a carbon is that the original of this is my monthly letter to Mary.

[At this point the writer tells his wife about reading my advertisement for the book, tells her that he hopes what he writes me will amuse her and stimulate her sexually and that she will masturbate and think of him. He says that what he has written has aroused him and he has masturbated a number of times in the course of the writing.]

You are lying in bed thinking of me. You're naked. You think about my cock and become mildly aroused. You touch your breasts, squeeze them gently until they begin to get firm. You lick your fingers and roll your nipples between them. They increase in size and by now you know you will masturbate. You put your fingers in the jar of Vaseline beside the cot and smear your nipples with it. After a few minutes of this, you feel the spreading dampness between your legs and you begin touching yourself there.

You hold the labia apart with the fingers of your left hand and put two fingers inside yourself with the other. You move your fingers around in a circle and in and out at the same time. Because your cunt is so big, you have never been able to bring yourself to orgasm manually. To have an orgasm you need a large cock inside you (like mine) or a dildo of some kind. The variety of dildos you have used in your life is numerous and creative. Candles, bottles, cucumbers, broom handles, chair legs, lollipops, hairbrush handles, bananas, rubber bicycle handle grips, doorknobs, a slipper, the gold lighter, those Tinker Toy connecting things, and heaven knows what else.

While you finger-fuck yourself, you're thinking about trying something new. Your cunt is open now, and you're making it bigger by making the circles bigger with your fingers. The car. The stick shift of the Porsche 111. The big mahogany knob on the end of the shift. It's a good size for you. Bigger than me, and longer. You get out of bed, fingers still inside of you, and look out the tent. Everybody is asleep, and the fire is low. You go to the car and open the door as quietly as possible. You get in and silently shut the door behind you. The car is in neutral, the gearshift is sticking straight up. You're in the back seat, kneeling. You bend over, your head between the seats, and take the knob in your mouth. You feel its hardness and roundness and you think of me. You pretend to yourself that I am there with you and that you are in the process of sucking me off. You're still masturbating.

It's not me you're sucking and the gearshift can't give you any of my ejaculata, which you love so dearly, and you soon tire of your fantasy. You crawl between the seats and position yourself over the shift. One hand is on the steering wheel and the other is on the dash. Slowly, you lower yourself onto the warm, wet knob. You've misjudged your position and you come to rest on the knob, not with your beautiful blond pussy, but on your lovely puckered asshole. There's still some Vaseline on your fingers and they're still wet from being inside you. You reach down under yourself and wipe on the Vaseline. You lower yourself onto the knob and pause briefly, taking its measure. Yes, you think, I'm girl enough to accommodate this rod.

You move yourself in a tiny circle, stretching the sphincter slightly. You lower yourself, little by little, making yourself larger, and bit by bit, the knob rises into you. A quarter of the way in, then half (you never thought you could stretch so much), and then you shrink in size as you sink down the bottom half of the knob.

And then you get a magnificent surprise. You sink down beyond the knob onto the chromium-plated shaft of the gearshift. It's icy cold and altogether thrilling. You've never felt anything as exciting as this in your life. It's maddeningly good.

The stick is about a foot long. You want all of it, every marvelous centimeter. Are you girl enough to take a foot of wood and cold steel up inside you? Inventive experimentalist that you are, you try. Lower and lower you sink, wishing the great iciness inside you were me. Higher and higher the shaft rises into you. It feels better than anything else you've ever had in you, except me.

As you descend, you masturbate with both hands. You've almost got the whole length inside you now. The fuzz from the floor will begin tickling your beautiful white bottom in a second or so. By God, you've done it. All the way down to the floor. You're proud of your accomplishment. You begin your ascent. When you get the whole thing out of you, knob and all, you fall on your glorious stick and take its entire length in one smooth and graceful motion. Up and down you go, kneeling and squatting and masturbating. Faster and faster you go. Up and down, up and down. The little car rocks to the rhythm of your joy. Squeak, squeak, squeak, go the springs. But, in your happiness, you don't hear their protest. The only thing you need now to complete your happiness is a cock the size of mine in your mouth.

Good as the slippery stick feels up inside your ass, up inside your lovely cunt will be better. Anal sex has always been fun for you, but just preliminary fun. The real thing for you, what brings you off best and most satisfyingly, is something big and wet rammed into you from the front. You kneel straight up, as in church, and the rod leaves you with a little slurping sound.

You're in a hurry now for an orgasm, or maybe two. The knob nestles against your wet blondness. It slips into you easily. You'll have to be careful from now on. You know you can't take a foot inside yourself there. My nine and a half inches is about maximum for you. Careful, careful. Oh my, it's good for you. Deeper and deeper it sinks into your warm, mysterious depth. Miracle of miracles! You are resting on the floor! You've taken it all, and it's heavenly.

If only you had a real live cock to suck while you ride your wild stallion.

This is fantasyland, my love, and miracles are quite ordinary here. My every wish for you is fulfilled merely by wishing it.

Your bouncing has again set the springs to singing. You have awakened the entire camp with your happy exertions. In your transports, you have not noticed that the car is surrounded by men, masturbating as they watch you. You finally do notice them after a big white blob of come splashes onto the windshield, just inches from your hungry mouth. You stop bouncing up and down on your giant automotive penis, you come to rest on the floor, hiding the great steel bar inside you. You hang your head in confusion, embarrassment, and shame. That the head of the expedition is an ordinary mortal with a fine, healthy sex drive has never occurred to the men before. They are amazed and pleased. Splash. More come on the windshield. Why are they doing this, you wonder. Why are they wasting their delicious seed on the cold and uncaring glass. You have a mouth and an asshole that need filling, you have hands that can masturbate two stalwarts at once. You have two large breasts that cry out for the feel of splashes of hot come. You have a face that yearns to be drenched in the beautiful stuff that is so good for the complexion. Splash. Another wasted wad.

The sight of all those men surrounding the car and jerking off arouses you to the point that you forget your embarrassment. It is normal for men to become aroused and masturbate at the sight of a large, luscious blond women masturbating. You remember that you are in charge here. These men work for you. They will do your bidding out of respect for your judgment and compassion for your great need.

You throw open both doors of the car. You tell the men exactly what you want. One man climbs into the back and puts his large and meaty cock up your hot ass. Other men take the top down. They stand on the hood with their cocks pointed at you. One man climbs in front with you and stands between you and the windshield. His glans smells salty and he comes (and you greedily swallow it all) after you give him one of those beautiful sucks of yours. As soon as he has finished, he leaves and is replaced by another. This is one of the men who came on the windshield and he lets you suck on him for a long time before presenting you with his wonderful-tasting come. When you've drunk all he has, you get still another and another.

You are completely surrounded by masturbating men. One man sits on the seat to your right and another on the seat to your left. You move their foreskins rapidly back and forth. Their swollen pricks are pointed at your nipples. Their come splashes warmly on your hard little nipples. Every now and then, someone comes and it falls on you like a tropical rain. Into your lovely face they come, and into your soft, blond hair. They come on your back and shoulders, and it drips down, like a river, into the crack of your ass. You wish you could drink it all, all the fine stuff they are squirting all over you as you bounce and suck and drink and masturbate the men.

This is the finest night of your life, marred only by the circumstance of my absence. You console yourself that I am there with you in spirit. Before the night is out, you have sucked every single man off, you have masturbated them all, each has had you up the ass and each has come on some part of your body. Do they never tire? Do they never run out of come to give you? Are the fires of their desire never quenched? And you, my love, doesn't your cunt get sore and your jaws tired and your asshole rubbed raw? No, no, no, to all these questions! You are both inexhaustible and insatiable. This is warfare. By the time you're through with these fortunate men, each will be a pale, sweating, hollow-eyed hulk, palsied of limb and red of tiny, limp, and wrinkled cock. You will have made each man come until he thinks he can stand it no longer, and then you will have shown him that you can bring him off again and again and yet again.

A man presents you with his cock. He pleads with you not to suck him off again. It is impossible for him to get it up again, he tells you, he has no more for you to drink. You fall on the dead organ like a vampire. Your lusty sucking (I can hear the loud slurpings) brings the tiny thing to life, and you feel its feeble stirrings on your swiftly moving tongue. The cock, protesting, rises and falls. The man groans with pain, but you show him no mercy. He will have an orgasm! He will! He will! You suck harder and harder, and finally, at last, you make him come. It's just a drop, to be sure, and his last drop at that. But you got it. The man staggers out of your mouth. He falls back a few feet from you and collapses on the ground. Another man pleads with you and tells you he can stand it no more. If he comes again, he tells you, he believes he will die. "Give me that cock!" you tell him sternly. Obediently, he gives it to you. You have been sucking for hours now, and the sun stands high in the sky and his cock stands high in your mouth until he comes his tiny droplet.

He wobbles away from you, clutching his chest. He falls to the ground, dead. All through the day, you suck and suck, until there is no come left in the camp. By sundown, you are in the center of a circle of unconscious or dead or dying men. You have beaten them all. For yourself, you have had twenty hours of nonstop orgasm and, for a change, all the come you can drink. For the first time in your life, you're entirely satisfied. You lie down and sleep. You deserve the rest.

Wouldn't it be lovely if things like this could come true? * * * *

There is more to anthropology, apparently, than I had supposed.

WHITE WOMEN LOVE IT ORALLY, YOU KNOW

This man wrote me a long, breezy letter filled with as fine a collection of misspellings as I have ever seen. He gave me the story of his life, told me about his wife, his job, his anxieties, fears, and ambitions, and, finally, after having introduced himself, he told me his fantasy. He's had it for years. He has it before and during intercourse with his wife.

* * * * My wife is black. So am I. When I say she's black, I mean black. Black as midnight, she is, and as beautiful as the sky. She's one fine woman. I wish I could tell her this fantasy, but I can't. She's a terrible prude. She's not a prude about sex. She's just a prude about talking about it. If she knew I was writing this, she'd die. And if she

knew about my fantasies, she'd really die. What I fantasize about is group sex. I've never had any, but I'd really love to. I'm never going to get any either because I don't cheat on her and I don't plan to. So the only way I'll get group sex is with a group that does not include her. And I just would feel terrible about doing sex if she were not there.

But I think about group sex a lot. Here's the scenario. I walk into my bedroom and my wife is in bed with a white woman. They're sixty-nining like mad and loving it. They don't see me standing there in the door, and I get to watch them for a little while. I watch them thrashing around on the bed and listen to them talk to each other and moan and groan and give each other directions and tell each other how great it is. Then they see me. They spring apart, both looking guilty as hell. I walk into the room, and I can tell by the look in their eyes that they're terrified. They think I'm angry and that I'm going to do something violent. But I'm not angry. I've been hoping for years that this would happen, and it finally has. I'm not angry. I'm horny.

I walk to the bed and stand next to it. I take out my cock and it's huge. My real life cock is big enough, but in the fantasy it's something else. It's as big as my forearm. And all during the fantasy it keeps getting bigger. I pull the white woman over to me and shove this huge cock into her mouth. It's so big I can hardly get it in. White women really love it orally, you know, and she helps me get it in. I can tell from the way she sucks on it that she's had lots of experience. The cock keeps growing and she keeps getting it all down. She gives me the granddaddy of all blow jobs, and when she's through, I give her the biggest wad I've ever unloaded. I give her so much she gags.

Well, my wife has been watching all this and she's mad. She can tell from all my groaning and carrying on that I have just been given the greatest blow job of all time. She shoves the white woman aside and takes my cock in her mouth. Now, that white woman was good, but she's nothing compared to my wife. She goes at that cock of mine like a crazy woman. She sucks and licks and nibbles; she talks to it and sings to it and rubs it and strokes it but most of all she sucks. And when I come, I come like a stallion. My hips are going back and forth like pistons and I'm roaring like a bull. Next to this blow job, the white woman's, for all her practice, is nothing.

Heterosexual Fantasies 65

Well, after two fine blow jobs, back to back, you'd think I'd be exhausted. But I'm not. I'm just getting started. I get out of my clothes and get into that bed and show them what fucking is all about. I fuck the regular way, up their asses, in their mouths, between their tits, and between their thighs. I fuck them standing and sitting and lying and running and jumping. I fuck them for hours without mercy. They're both screaming with happiness. Nobody in the world has ever fucked anybody like I'm fucking these two ladies.

And along about now, in real life, I come. I really love that fantasy and my wife does, too, even though she doesn't know I have it. If I didn't have that fantasy I couldn't fuck her as good as I do. * * * *

BLACK LIPS, BLACK PUSSY

In my work I use a Sony TC-110 tape recorder and C-60 tapes. The tape recorder has a counter on it that tells how much tape has been used and how much tape there is left. At the end of an interview, I write the number on the counter on the cassette along with the name of whomever I interviewed. At the end of a fashionable Hollywood party I went into a bedroom and got my coat and picked up the Sony. I noted that the number on the counter was advanced some three hundred units ahead of when I put it there hours earlier. Someone had been recording on the machine for about twenty minutes. When I got back to my hotel, I backed the reel to its original setting and listened. I think I recognize the voice but I'm not sure. The din from the party going on in the next room makes it almost impossible to tell who it is, but if it's who I think it is, he has an Academy Award.

* * * * Paul tells me you're doing a book on men's sexual fantasies. What a hell of a great subject. I don't think anybody has done a book like this before. Good luck with it.

I've recently completed three years of analysis. Three years ago, I could never tell anybody my fantasies. I was terribly uptight about sex. Even now I would find it hard to tell you face to face, which is why I'm here in the john talking to your Sony.

I'm a white man. divorced and thinking about getting married again. My first wife was white. My second, if she marries me, will also be white. But I have this crazy thing about black chicks. I fuck them every chance I get, which is a lot of chances. My dreams are almost exclusively about black women, and my fantasies are exclusively about black ladies. I'm from the South. Maybe that has something to do with it. Black women were forbidden when I was growing up. Maybe that's what makes them so mysterious and attractive to me.

In my fantasies I see myself kissing full black lips. They taste sweet. They smell like milk. I'm getting aroused as I tell you this. The woman kisses me. I touch her close-cropped hair. She is a black woman from Africa. She's wearing a long dashiki. She has no underwear underneath. I feel her wonderfully small hard breasts push against my chest. I move my pelvis forward. I feel her tremble when my penis shoves against her through my pants. She begins to breathe hard. She fumbles around my fly and gets it open, releasing my penis. There is a drop of clear liquid on the end of it. She kneels in front of me and holds my cock gently between her thumb and forefinger. She guides my cock to her mouth. She licks off the drop of liquid and looks up at me and smiles. "I'm going to suck you dry," she says.

She sucks on me for hours. Sometimes she sucks hard, and sometimes she sucks gently. Sometimes she just sucks the head of my cock, and sometimes she takes the entire shaft into her mouth. When she does that, my cock is way down her throat. She swallows rapidly when I'm in her deep. The swallowing movements in her throat make my cock feel so good I almost can't stop myself from coming. She senses that I am about to come and squeezes me hard with her thumb and forefinger. This beautiful black lady really loves my cock. She's the greatest cocksucker I've ever known.

There's a glass of whiskey on the rocks near by. She stops sucking my cock for a moment and takes a big drink from the glass. She does not swallow. She puts my cock back in her mouth. It feels so cold and so good that my toes curl up, and involuntarily my pelvis starts rocking back and forth. She puts her hands on the cheeks of my ass and pushes me hard into her. The cock goes down her throat deeper than before. Her nose is buried in my pubic hair. She opens her mouth wide and gets the upper part of my scrotum in her mouth. With her fingers, she pushes my balls in. The ice-cold whiskey on my balls feels so good I goddamn near pass out.

She takes me out of her mouth. I am shaking all over like a wet dog. Her mouth is about six inches from the head of my cock. She blows on it. The evaporating whiskey makes my cock feel cold. She moves the foreskin slowly back and forth. I'm so excited that I can hardly speak, but I manage to gasp that I'm going to come. I can't stop myself. Her fingers keep moving my foreskin back and forth and I come like a fucking railroad train. I've never come like that before. Spurt, spurt, spurt. Spasm after spasm flying that six inches between the end of my cock and her open mouth. The spasms get smaller and weaker. She puts my cock back in her mouth and sucks hard. When we're through, she has sucked me dry. My cock hangs there all limp and happy.

By the time I get to this point in the fantasy, I'm ready to come. I very rarely masturbate, but when I do, this is the fantasy I like best. When I'm fucking a girl and I'm having a hard time holding an erection, usually because I'm tired after a day's shooting or because I have had too much booze, I use this fantasy to keep my pecker up. It's never failed me yet.

Good luck with the book. I hope you can use this. I like seeing myself in print.

Oh, sometimes I see myself going down on black ladies. The feel of their pubic hair is much different from white women's. A lot of white people think that a black woman's pubic hair is coarse like Brillo. It's not. It's springy and nice.

The pussy of a black woman is dark and mysterious to look at. Very exciting. Not more exciting than a white woman's, but different and exciting in a different way.

The woman dressed in the dashiki, by the way, is an actual woman. In real life she has blown me many times. But never in exactly the way I imagine in the fantasy. * * * *

I HAVE THIS THING FOR BLACK WOMEN

* * * * Ever since I was a kid, I've had this fantasy about black women. I'm in a room with ten of them. One is French-kissing me, another is sucking my cock, another is licking my asshole, two are nibbling on my toes, two are running their tongues around in my ears, I'm finger-fucking two, and the last one is walking around with a mirror so I can see everything that's going on. I don't know any of the women. They're not whores. They do this for me because I have such a great body. Actually my body isn't all that great, but in my fantasies, I'm a regular Charles Atlas with a cock like an axe handle. Long and smooth and straight and hard. * * * *

WIDOWER

* * * * My wife died several years ago, after forty years of marriage. I'm very lonely. I hire girls to put a vibrator in me and hold me in their arms and tell me they love me. I don't come very often anymore. But when the girl holds me, I think of my wife, and I'm happy for a while.

I hire girls to take me for walks. We get into the park and I unzip my fly. There is a necktie tied to my penis. The girl leads me through the park as if I were her pet. I don't know why I like this, but I do, when people see us and look at us funny. * * * *

One of my friends told me this one. He's not an old man. He says he thinks he read it somewhere.

UNDRESSING

* * * * The biggest turn on for me is watching a girl undress. First the topcoat, then her suit jacket, blouse, bra, skirt, panties, panty hose, and shoes. There she stands before me in the eye of my mind in all her female glory. She turns to me and smiles, and although I don't

know her, I know I love her and she loves me. This isn't much of a fantasy, I know. But it pleases me to think about it. It doesn't arouse me as much as it just makes me happy to think about it. * * * *

The number of incest fantasies reported was surprisingly low. "Surprisingly" because it is such a common crime and has been so for as long as men have been writing history and, without doubt, before then. Many of my friends have nubile daughters and are quite blunt about the difficulties they have keeping their hands off them. In most cases they have communicated their problem to their wives or daughters and the child makes it easier on the old man by not giving him wet, sloppy kisses and sitting on his lap whenever the opportunity arises. One of my friends, a widower with a nineteen-year-old daughter who drove him to sexual distraction, asked me, several years ago, to speak to her about the matter. She told me that she had wanted her father to bed her for all her adolescence and that she tempted him on purpose, believing that he did not notice her enticing behavior and she was therefore somehow "safe." She took mercy on her father, a lawyer, and shortly after our discussion she married a man who looks and acts remarkably like her father and is also a lawyer. The young man works in her father's firm and will one day, doubtless, inherit it. Her father, meanwhile, has married again. His new wife is remarkably like his first. His daughter is also very much like her mother. This situation, it seems to me, is as close to incest as one can get within the bounds of legality.

ELECTRA

* * * * My daughter just turned eighteen. I have a lech for her you just wouldn't believe. Sometimes just being in the same room with her alone is so sexually stimulating for me, I just have to leave the room and go to the bathroom and jerk off while thinking about what I wish she would do to me.

My wife goes to the store and Margaret and I are alone. We're just sitting in the living room making small talk. I get very aroused. But I'm interested in what we're talking about and I forget to leave the room. I've got a real throbber on. My cock bulges in my pants, and every once in a while I have a sort of spasm and my fly jumps.

After a while, I notice that we're not talking anymore and she seems agitated. She's breathing heavily and looking at everything in the room except me. Finally she asks me in a very tiny voice, "What are you thinking about, daddy?"

"Honey," I tell her, "you don't really want to know. I'm thinking something terrible that I can't tell you about."

She slumps back in her chair, the way teen-agers do, and lets her legs sprawl like they do when they're wearing jeans. Except she's not wearing jeans. I can see the darkness of her between her legs. She's still looking everywhere but at me, but I can't take my eyes from between her legs.

"I'm not a virgin, daddy, and haven't been since last summer. When I am with a boy and he's loving me, I pretend to myself that he's you. Sometimes, at night, I hear you and momma making love. I masturbate and try to imagine what the two of you are doing, and I pretend that what you are doing, you are doing to me."

"Honey," I tell her, "what you're talking about is incest. It's the most horrible crime there is. Worse than murder, worse than anything."

"A lot of my girl friends have been having sex with their fathers for years. Some of the fathers are friends of yours. One of them is a very good friend. He and Kathy have had sex together almost every day since she was thirteen. She loves it and she loves him. They're just a father and a daughter who are making each other very happy and not causing anybody any harm."

(Kathy's father, Jim, is one of my oldest and closest friends. He's just one helluva nice guy. A real straight guy, honest, hard-working, we go to the same church.)

"I've never seen your penis. I know you have a hard on now. If I promise to stay where I am, will you show it to me? Then, when I think about you, I'll know and not be just guessing. Please? I'll stay right here. I won't budge. I swear."

What the hell, I tell myself. There can't be any harm in letting her look at it. I unzip and show it to her. She's not looking around the room anymore, I can tell you. She's looking at me like I was the Mona Lisa. All sort of adoring and awestruck.

"I've seen three pricks in my life, but none were as big as that. Lucky momma. Do you let her suck it?"

At the mention of the word "suck," my cock starts throbbing up and down, and it's all I can do to keep my hands off it. She pulls her panties down and starts playing with herself. I can see the glistening of her moisture, and I think I can smell the smell of her.

"I'm pretending that beautiful thing of yours is up inside me," she says, still looking at it as if hypnotized. "I promised I wouldn't budge and I won't. But if you'll let me, I'd like to come over and look at it up close. I promise I won't touch."

I'm so excited I can't speak. I just nod my head weakly, and she comes over to my chair, all slow and woman-like, like her mother, and kneels down in front of me. She doesn't touch me, all right, but she's so close to me, I can feel her breath on it, and I can smell her, strong and good.

"Will you take your pants down a little so I can see everything you have?"

I undo my belt and unbutton the top button and slip my pants down. I have to raise up a little to do this. The tip of my cock is all wet by this time, and it touches her lips, leaving a little spot of wetness. We both gasp when this happens and she's getting a wild sort of look in her eyes. Her chest is heaving at this point and so is mine.

She licks her lips. "Ummmmmmmmmmm," she moans as she licks. She looks into my eyes. I can see the longing and the hunger there. Bottomless, animal, desperate. She's trembling and her fingers inside herself are making little sucking noises. She opens her mouth wide and starts licking her lips, now all puffy with desire, and making sucking noises. She opens her mouth as wide as she can and bows over me. I can't help myself. I'm only human. I start coming. It shoots great pearly spurts into her mouth.

"Honey, *please,*" I groan. And down she goes on me, sucking like an angel. I just can't seem to stop coming. I've never had an orgasm like this one. And the more I come, the harder she sucks, until I have no more to give her. I let go of her head. Her nose is hard up against my hair. As she withdraws from me, she is sucking harder than I have ever been sucked before and moving her tongue rapidly back and forth. She withdraws very, very slowly. By the time her lips leave the head, I am beginning to get erect again.

"Thank you, daddy," she says, looking at my erection beginning to rebuild, "I have never sucked a real man before. You've ruined the boys for me forever. Are you ready for me to do it again? Do you want to do something else? Would you like to be inside me?"

While she's saying this, she stands up in front of me, hiking up her skirts so I can see her fingers working inside herself, see her juices run down her fingers and drip off the knuckles. It's almost unbearably beautiful. Those child-woman's hands stimulating that fabulously beautiful, innocent pussy. I put my arms around her hips and draw her to me, to my mouth. I press into her hard, I almost suffocate in the goodness of her. I suck on her hard and move my mouth around in a circle. She's groaning in ecstasy and pumping herself into me. It just takes a few seconds for her to climax. My mouth feels the sudden loosening of her and I drink her juices, all of them I can get. She collapses on top of me, panting.

I look at my watch. Her mother has been gone for about an hour. Saturday shopping takes her at least two hours. I kick my trousers off and carry her upstairs to her bedroom in my arms as I did when she was a child. She's warm and relaxed in my arms and nestles and nips on my neck as we go up.

I lay her on the bed and take my clothes off. I take off her skirt and blouse and bra. She's lying there smiling adoringly at me, looking at my prick and wondering how it's going to feel inside her. I walk across the hall to my bedroom and get a rubber out of the top drawer. She looks at it when I come in and shakes her head in distaste. "I'm on the pill," she says.

I lie on top of her between her legs and suck her large firm breasts.

Heterosexual Fantasies   73

She moves her hips in a circle under me. So far I have not committed incest, I tell myself. That requires actual penetration, legally. She's writhing under me, getting my stomach wet. My prick is throbbing hard again. She wants me inside her, my prick is dying to go inside her, but my head is screaming *no*.

I raise up, letting her breast fall from my lips, and move up to her so that we are now nose to nose. My prick is in a terrible state now, slapping up against her between her legs and feeling her heat and wetness. "Honey," I begin, "I just can't bring myself to do it. What we've done so far is bad enough. If I do what we both want to do, it will change our whole lives. We'll hate each other and ourselves until the day we die."

As I'm saying this, she holds my balls in one hand and my prick in the other, and she convulsively moves her hips and plunges me deep inside her. All is lost. I am fucking my own daughter and loving it. Our rhythms exactly match. She's tight and hotter there than my wife. Her hands are on my shoulders and she's looking into my eyes as we bang against each other with hard thrusts that increase in intensity and speed until, to an observer, our bodies must have been a blur. Faster and faster we go. Her whimpers change to throaty groans, and I feel her orgasm begin to rise and grow, and from her face, I know the pleasure I am giving her, and I come in great shuddering spasms until I collapse on top of her, spent and trembling all over. She puts her arms around me and hugs me. She loves me, she is saying, and I love her and everything will be all right. * * * *

MORE INCEST

* * * * The fact of the matter is that, when we were children, little children, eight or nine or so, my younger sister (by a year) and I used to fool around a little. She used to take down her pants and let me look at her, both front and back, and I used to do the same thing for her. We used to play doctor with the other kids in the neighborhood. Nobody touched anybody, as I remember it, we just looked at each other. The high point of my prepubescence occurred when a little girl put a clothespin inside herself and let all the guys touch it.

My sister used to come in the bathroom and watch me pee, and I used to do the same thing, squatting down in front of her so I could watch it run out. Kid stuff and harmless.

We're both in our forties now. She lives on the East Coast and I live on the West. We're both married. We see each other maybe once a year. The last time I saw her was about two months ago. Our mother died and I went East for the funeral. I spent the night at her house. She doesn't have any children. Her husband is a CPA and it was tax time. About half the time, from March 15 to April 15, he sleeps over in his office, and despite the funeral, this was one of those nights. My sister and I slept in the same house alone. Before going to sleep, I had the following fantasy, which led to a lovely erection, masturbation, and a sound night's sleep.

Before the funeral, we had a couple of drinks to fortify ourselves against the upcoming barbarities. Her husband drove us home afterwards and took off for the office. Four or five friends came over for drinks and stayed for hours and hours and finally, one by one, drifted away, leaving the two of us alone. By this time, both of us were about half drunk.

I went to the toilet and neglected to close the door. She heard me splashing away and came to the doorway to look. She remarked that I had grown. She told me not to flush it, she had to go herself. What the hell, I figured, she'd watched me so I might as well watch her. I squatted down and looked at her. "So have you," I said.

When she was finished, we went back to the bar for a nightcap, and I told her the truth. Having her watch me and my watching her had turned me on. I didn't have a hard on or anything, but I had that good feeling in my lower stomach. That's what I told her.

I stood behind the bar and she sat on a stool in front of it. She unbuttoned her blouse and pulled down the front of her bra. "I've grown here, too," she said, and her boobs came spilling out. Wow! I'll say she'd grown. She put her bra back in place and started buttoning the blouse. I asked her if she'd mind not doing that. I asked her if she'd unbutton and pull down the bra again so I could look at her while we finished our drink. She said that I must be a mind reader. She wanted me to look at her. She liked her breasts and thought they were beautiful. Henry, her husband, paid no attention to them. At her age, she said, they were not going to stay pretty for too many more years. She'd like them to be appreciated before they started to sag.

She was explaining this as she unbuttoned and pulled the bra down again.

Her breasts are large and full with prominent pink nipples and a large pink area surrounding. A big, blue vein was prominent in each. They pulsed with her heartbeat. We talked for a while and decided to have another drink.

The bar is in the living room. There is a big picture window and the venetian blinds were up. Neighbors looking in would see nothing out of the way because her back was to the window. I asked her if I could touch her breasts. She said, "Sure." She buttoned up again and shut the blinds and turned out the lights. A moment later a match flared and she lighted a candle at the end of the bar. Her clothes were in a heap in the middle of the floor. She was completely naked. After she lit the candle, she put the chain on the door so Henry could not surprise us. The phone rang. It was Henry calling to say goodnight. He was about to turn in for a couple of hours sleep before beginning the grind again. They've been married for nearly twenty years and they still talk like lovers.

While they said goodnight, I stripped. I had about as big a hard on as a drunk can get. Which is to say, it got thick and pointed at about a forty-five degree angle to the floor. An instance of the flesh being willing, but the spirit weak. Or the spirit willing and the flesh weak.

She couldn't see this because I was still behind the bar.

The telephone was on the wall at the far end of the bar. When they finished talking, she came back to the bar stool in front of me and sat down and leaned over so I could touch her. I put both hands, palm up, on the bar. She placed a large, warm gland in each and we looked at each other and beamed with happiness. She liked me to hold them and told me so, and I liked doing it and told her so.

We began talking about our sex lives, hers with Henry and mine with Gwen, and occasional side affairs. She wondered if Henry had affairs. I knew he did but I kept my mouth shut. I took my hand off one of her boobs and took a drink from my glass. On impulse, I put her breast in the glass getting it wet with scotch and soda. I leaned over and licked it off. She giggled. My hard on improved a little.

"Are you getting aroused?" she asked.

I stepped back so she could see.

"Put it over the sink and run cold water on it and it'll go away." I did as she asked and it didn't go away. I filled a glass pitcher with ice and water, and in a minute or so, it shrivelled. I began emptying the pitcher. She took it out of my hand and drank from it. We went back to talking about our sex lives. She asked me if Gwen liked oral sex, and I told her the truth. Gwen doesn't like it, she loves it. A regular vampire, a cormorant.

I had to explain that a cormorant is a diving bird. I had to explain that a diving bird means a girl who goes down.

She said that Henry wouldn't let her. Early in their marriage she had tried and he had been aghast and said that was something only whores and queers do. She was so ashamed she'd never tried it again. She knew from listening to her friends that all of them went down on their husbands frequently. She'd never had the nerve to tell Henry this. She thought about it a lot, and sometimes while she masturbated with one peeled cucumber, she sucked on another. It gave her some satisfaction doing this, she said, but not a lot. A cucumber is the right size and it's wet. But it's also cool, and a cock is hot.

I was leaning against the bar, touching her breasts once in a while, pouring booze on them and licking them. My cock was big again and parallel to the floor, an improvement of forty-five degrees.

I wanted to ask her if she wanted to suck me but I didn't have the nerve. Without thinking about it, I reached down and started stroking myself. She saw what I was doing and leaned over to watch. "You're bigger than Henry," she said, "and it's not all the way up yet. If you're going to make yourself come, do it in the sink."

I stopped touching myself and stayed where I could touch her and give her a little suck once in a while. She said, "If you want to make yourself come, I want to watch." This shocked us both and we drank in silence for a few minutes and my erection went away.

I fixed more drinks.

"Does she let you do it in the back?"

"We tried it once. I got just a part of the head in. It hurt, she said, and we never tried it again. Or we think we never tried it again. We went to a party one night and got terribly drunk. She woke up the next day with a very sore rear. She examined my cock, which was very red, and smelled it. It smelled like my cock always smells after sex, she said. I may have done it to her in the behind first and in the usual way the second time, but neither of us is sure."

I guess talking about smells triggered something in her. She put her hand between her legs and put her fingers under my nose. Her fingers were very wet and her smell was very strong. She smelled her own fingers and made a face. I rinsed the bar rag thoroughly in warm water and handed it to her. She cleaned herself out and gave it back. I rinsed it again. She put her fingers inside herself and put them under my nose. They smelled fine and I sucked on them and held her breasts while she talked about herself and Henry.

Henry liked the missionary position, liked her to squat so he could get into her from the rear, liked her to stand on the floor with her legs spread and lean against a wall so he could get into her that way. They did it in the shower and bathtub and once did it while swimming. Once when she was squatting for him, he fell out, he was going so fast. She reached up (she had been holding his balls) to help him back in, misjudged where he was, and he wound up squarely in her rear. She came instantly. It didn't hurt. Quite the contrary, it felt wonderful. Henry, of course, was all apologetic and remorseful. She didn't tell him how good it was for her. She's tried it with cucumbers, but they're not stiff enough and break before she can get them in.

"Thank God for the ice pick handle," she said pointing to the ice pick with a plastic handle on the drain rack just under my cock, which was again parallel to the floor. She saw it, my cock, and smiled. I picked up the ice pick and sucked the handle. She spit on her hand and rubbed it on her rear, took the pick away from me and put it inside her. I asked her if I could see. I went around to her side of the bar and squatted down. She sat on the bar stool on one cheek and moved the handle slowly in and out. She played with her clitoris with her other hand, rolled it between her thumb and forefinger. I spread her cheeks wider to get an even closer look.

Very, very exciting. I was now about ten degrees above parallel. Little involuntary spasms made it bob up and down. I stroked myself and found that I was highly insensitive from all the Scotch. I doubted if I could masturbate myself to climax. I stroked back and forth anyway, enjoying what little sensation I could get. She watched me between her legs. "Get me something to suck on, please," she asked, looking hungrily at my cock.

I got up to go to the kitchen to get her a cucumber.

"Come back here, you idiot."

I climbed up on the bar and sat on it facing her with my legs hanging down. She started sucking me. I put my foot against her pussy and moved it up and down. She looked up at one point in her ministrations and said, "This sure beats hell out of cucumbers."

I don't know how long she sucked but she finally stopped. "It's nice, but I think I've got lockjaw. Can't you come? They say it's a good taste. I can go on for another few minutes if you think you can come for me."

She was sweating and her hair was stringy. Her face was red from her exertions. I told her I was too drunk to come. "What time will Henry get home?" I asked.

"He comes in around lunchtime for a quick bite, a piece of ass, a shower, and a change of clothes, and then he's off again."

"I can come for you in the morning, when I'm sober."

She was getting her breath back. "How about that other thing he doesn't like?" she asked, handing me the ice pick. I fixed us two more drinks and came around to her side of the bar. I led her to the middle of the room and lay down on my side. We decided to finish our drinks first. She lay beside me, her head near my cock. We talked and giggled about how bad we were. Every now and then she'd lean over and give it a good hard suck. Her mouth was cold. I knew, if she kept it up, I could probably come for her. We finished our drinks at the same time. "How do we go about this?" she wondered. I suggested we try the way Henry had gotten inside her.

She squatted on her hands and knees. I put myself up against her and pushed. She was dry and very tight. I put it in her pussy and rubbed against her to make her wet and tried again. I pushed hard and hurt myself a little. She got up and went to the kitchen and came back with a quarter-pound bar of butter. She rubbed me with it and handed it to me and turned around. I spread her and greased her up and, on impulse, shoved the butter up her cunt. She giggled and said she'd done that before. She took a towel from the bar, put it on the floor and got down on all fours on top of it. I put myself inside her front to see what the combination of her warmth and the cold butter would be. Nice. I took it out and slid it into her rear easily. Each time I went into her I pulled it out. All the way out, as I had seen her do with the ice pick handle. I pushed myself all the way in her as far as I could go. I pulled her hips into me and jerked my pelvis forward at the end of each stroke and then slowly withdrew, all the way out again.

The butter was oozing out as I went in.

I couldn't come before, but I felt the stirrings inside and knew I could come now. I didn't want to, I wanted to make it last. I told her I thought I could come and asked her if she wanted it there or in her mouth. She told me to go wash myself off and she'd take it in the mouth. I went to the john and cleaned myself with a soapy washcloth. She came in to pee and watch me. I poured water on myself, using the toothbrush glass, and when I swung around she grabbed my balls and pulled me into her mouth. I reached behind her and flushed the john. I asked her to take it easy so I could last a long time. She shook her head vigorously. "I've waited all my life to do this. I'm in a hurry. If I can, I'll do it twice, but right now I want you right now." And back in her mouth I went.

I told her Gwen was able to get all of me in her. She had been a champion beer-drinker in college and had taught herself to chug-a-lug a full bottle of beer without swallowing once. She just opened up her throat and poured the beer down. That's how she got the entire length of me in her mouth. She just opened her throat and in it all went.

She tried it and gagged, tried again, gagged again, tried a third time and down it went, all the way. She rolled her eyes up at me and crinkled them at me. She was proud of herself and she liked it. I told her to swallow hard four or five times and I would be able to come, I thought. She pushed me away gently. She told me she wanted me to come in her mouth so she could taste it. She turned around on the john seat and filled the waterpick with warm water and shoved it inside herself. "I'll do the swallowing thing, but when you feel yourself starting, make sure just the head is in my mouth." Back in and all the way down I went. She swallowed five or six times, and I felt it coming on me in a rush. I pulled out so she could taste, and she turned the waterpick on. It was a nice, long, slow, leisurely orgasm, one spasm following on the heels of another like breakers against a shore, one following the other in mindless primordial rhythm.

This is the place where I whacked off and went to sleep.

I've changed the names and the circumstances under which we slept together under the same roof alone, but enough of what I've said is close enough to the reality that, if she read this, she might recognize it. I'm fantasizing now that she does read it, does recognize it, and calls me on the phone and tells me she was thinking the same things that night and would like to try it in real life. I wonder what I'd do? * * * *

I don't know why, but these incest fables don't bother me at all. I have a half-sister and my progeny are all sons. Maybe that has something to do with it. The Pharaohs kept it all in the family for generation after generation as a religious duty and godly (they being the gods) necessity without effect, ill or otherwise. In our own time, there are various primitive tribes that still regard the practice as harmless.

2

HOMOSEXUAL FANTASIES

MUHAMMAD AND THE HOOKER

This one was phoned into my machine by a drunken bartender friend of mine. He doesn't know to this day that I know it was he who called it in. If he knew I knew, he would probably shrivel with embarrassment. He's very Irish and very Catholic, married, and has about ten kids. I have a friend, the English sexologist Robert Chartham whose lecherous voice carries fifty yards. Chartham was discussing anal sex one day with me in the Irish workingman's saloon where my bartender friend worked. Chartham forgets, occasionally, that many people are not quite as uninhibited about sex as he is. In his marvelous haw-haw voice he was saying something about not forgetting to wash one's penis before and after a session of anal sex. The entire bar turned around to look at him—the looks were mostly horrified. Whether the horror was because there was an Englishman in their midst, or whether they were scandalized by the subject he was embarked on, I don't know—but I do know that Billy, the bartender, picked up a bottle by its neck and started to move in our direction. I hustled Doctor Chartham from the bar and probably saved his life and the contents of a bottle of good whiskey.

* * * * I am standing on the sidewalk in front of Xaviera Hollander's apartment house. I am pissing into her gas tank. While I am doing that Muhammad Ali sneaks up behind me and snatches down my pants. He begins fucking me up the ass. While he's doing that, it begins to snow. Fireworks are going off all around us. When Ali is finished with me, he carefully washes off his penis in the snow. * * * *

ASS MAN

* * * * I am twenty-four, gay (still in the closet), a graduate student at a large university in Pennsylvania, and I think about asses and assholes all the time. The asses and the assholes are uniformly beautiful. They are always covered with tiny red freckles. The assholes are all clean and they have a fine musky smell to them. Just like mine. I daydream about asses all the time. At night in my dreams, I dream about them. One fantasy I have all the time is that my lover puts his whole arm up inside me and then his head. His arm moves in and out, and his head is licking and chewing away on me. In real life, he does get part of his arm in me.

Most of the time I see myself looking at the freckled ass of an eighteen-year-old boy. The ass is very close to me, but the asshole is hidden. I spread his cheeks and there the beautiful thing is, all rosy and clean. I kiss it. This thrills him. He pushes his asshole at me and I lick it. I lick it for a long time to get the muscles relaxed so that my tongue can slip in and out easily. When I first start tonguing, I can only get a little of it in, but as time goes by and my lover gets more excited and more relaxed and really wanting my tongue in him as far as I can get it, the asshole starts loosening up. The taste is delicious. I'd rather eat an asshole than food. An asshole is better than food. You can lick an asshole and stick your cock into it and come into it. You can't do that with food.

Next to kissing, licking, and sticking my tongue into assholes, I like to suck on them and stick my cock in them. The last thing I do is get my cock in. All the other things get done first. I like to put it in nice and slow and speed up as I go along. I am not gentle when I am fucking an asshole. I charge upon it with vigor, as Jack Kennedy used to say, and slam in and out of it for hours at a time. In my fantasies, I never get tired, and I can keep from coming for as long as my lover wishes. I love playing switch, which means pulling my cock out of his asshole and putting it immediately into his mouth, so he can suck it for a while, and then back into the asshole, and then back in the mouth, until I finally come. When I do this twice, if I came up his ass the first time, I come in his mouth the second and vice versa.

I love being sucked off, but it's not as good for me that way as coming up his ass. While he is sucking me, I shut my eyes and dream that what I am feeling is his nice, soft asshole rising and falling on my cock. My fantasy cock is gigantic. Whenever a man sees it, he wants it up his ass right away. I walk into a crowded train, into the first car. I take my huge cock out. I walk to the first man in the first seat. He is drinking a drink. I put my dick in it. One look and he wants it up his ass. He stands up, the pants come down, and he offers me his ass. The other men in the car see my wonderful cock giving him the greatest thrill he has ever had in his life. They start lining up, waiting their turns. The same thing happens in every car on the train. I get to fuck them all, even the conductors. The only men I don't fuck are the men in the engine. They've got to keep their minds on the tracks. But when the train stops at a station, I get them then. Passengers in the station see the performance and go wild for my cock. I oblige until the train starts to pull out. I apologize to those I couldn't help and jump on board again. The men in the train are frantic. They all want me to fuck them some more. All of them, all the way to California.

You should see what's bumping against the typewriter as I type this.

I have made a discovery. Writing about assholes is fun. Asshole. It's a beautiful word to look at. The *O* in *hole* is sexy. I think I'll lick it and pretend.

Marlon Brando and Paul Newman. I see myself with these two beauties sometimes. At the same time. While I'm fucking one, I'm tonguing the other. I can't stand it.

I'm sure you can guess what I just did. Just in case you're not very bright, the results of my activity were deposited on the previous page. When you get this, it will be dry. Give the page a sniff. I'm sure you'll recognize the smell. In case you're a eunuch and don't recognize the smell, it is come. Semen or sperm to you, the stuff that asses crave.

I'll just bet you're jerking off. In fact I just bet this book of yours is a jerk-off. Every letter you get, out comes the old pork and whackity-whack. I wish I had the nerve to call you on the telephone and find out how many times you've flogged the dog reading this. Think of all the sperm you're wasting, you naughty man. * * * *

THE HAIRY COWBOY

I don't know very much about this man except that he's twenty-five, homosexual, and a graduate student.

* * * * When I was eighteen, my older sister brought her boyfriend home for the first time. One look at the brute and I fell in love. He was a giant, a six-foot, seven-inch, hairy cowboy type. Every time I walked through the room I couldn't stop myself from looking at his crotch. I'd walk through the room, look at the bulge in his pants, and go upstairs and jerk off. Must have walked through that room ten times that night.

The boyfriend, in my fantasy, wants to get in good with my sister. He asks me if I like fishing, and I tell him yes. He suggests that we go on a weekend fishing trip. I tell him I'd love to go. He picks me up in a battered panel truck the next weekend and we drive to the mountains. He's wearing Levis, boots, and a great big Stetson. God, he looks great.

We get to the mountains and set up camp. We build a fire and cook dinner. After dinner, he strips down to his shorts and crawls into his sleeping bag. I get into mine. I'm frantic. I want to get in his sleeping bag so bad I can taste it. The night is noisy with a lot of animal noises. I call over to him across the fire and tell him I'm afraid. He does not answer. I tell him again that I'm afraid to sleep by myself in the open. He does not answer. He begins snoring. I decide I'll take a chance. I leave my sleeping bag and crawl into his. It's like being in a telephone booth with a bear. There's hardly room for him let alone me.

He does not wake up. I reach down between his legs and feel his sleeping penis. It's not as large as I had expected in so mountainous a specimen. I move the foreskin gently back and forth, and I feel the first stirrings of his little bird. I move my hand back and forth faster, and the little bird grows in my hand to monstrous proportions. It is positively the largest penis I have ever felt. I can barely get my hand around the thing. I didn't know humans came with penises like this, a great tree of a joint.

He wakes up and feels my hand working away. "So that's how you want it?" he says. He takes off his shorts and I see his mighty engine for the first time. Unbelievable. Long and thick and throbbing and altogether lovable. Surrounded by a forest of black hair. Beautiful. He motions me toward him. He pushes me to my knees. The great, beautiful cock is scant inches from my mouth. I wonder if I can get a cock that size inside. I get part of the head in and start sucking. The cock gets even bigger. He begins thrusting back and forth. His big hands are on either side of my head. As he thrusts forward, he pulls my head toward him roughly. My lips stretch, my jaw aches, but finally I've got the monster in my mouth. When he thrusts forward, the thing goes down my throat like a great slippery eel. God, it's good. I never had a cock this big before.

He comes. He doesn't come like any ordinary mortal. He comes like a god. He pumps and pumps his delicious come into me until I think I'm going to drown in it. I love it so much, I don't lose a drop of the lovely stuff. He finishes after a long time, and the monster becomes a little bird again. He closes his eyes and I fear he is going to sleep. I go over to him and put his cock in my mouth. It still tastes like come, and I suck and lick it all over to make sure I don't lose a drop. He gets big again. Just as big as before.

He takes my head between his hands and pulls me away. He rolls me over on my stomach and spreads my cheeks. He spits on his hand and lubricates my asshole with it. "Have you ever had it like this?" he asks. I tell him no. Suddenly I feel this searing, tearing pain, and he is in me all the way to the hilt. I scream with pain but he ignores the screams. He batters and bludgeons me. He rides me like a man on a bucking bronco. He thrusts and bashes into me again and again. I feel his balls coming up against my asshole. The pain is leaving me now, and all I feel is that great cock going into me and going out again. The pain leaves and it starts feeling good. My asshole has stretched to accommodate his great cock. Oh, it feels so good. And then he comes, and I feel the hot semen squirting into me. In a couple of seconds, he grows small and withdraws. He goes to sleep and I masturbate myself to sleep. We spend the rest of the weekend fucking and sucking. We do no fishing at all.

All this is fantasy. The guy is now married to my sister. Neither one of them knows I'm gay. * * * *

HOW YOU'RE GONNA KEEP HIM DOWN ON THE FARM

Like most of the fantasies in this collection, this one is a mixture of recollection and wish. I lived on a farm part of my boyhood. There were a dozen or so horses on the farm. I don't believe it is possible to have sex with a horse in the manner this caller describes. A pony, maybe—but not a horse.

* * * * My fantasy life and my real life are one and the same. I act all my sexual fantasies out, and after I act them out I fantasize about what I did. I have all kinds of automatic photography equipment and thousands of pictures of me with guys. Black guys really turn me on. I have pictures of me sucking their nipples, blowing them, licking assholes, and stuff like that. I have hundreds of photos of me masturbating. Many of these show the come shooting out. I look at pictures of me masturbating and I get all hot and I do masturbate. I have shots of me looking at pictures of me masturbating while I'm masturbating.

I have a collection of shots showing a guy fucking me, one guy sucking me, and me sucking somebody else. Artistic as hell. One interesting thing about these shots is that everybody is working on everybody else with dildos or vibrators. Ever notice people's faces when they come? It looks like they're in pain when actually they're feeling the greatest thing in the universe.

I have a more or less steady lover. He has a farm up in the country. I take my camera gear along. He takes my clothes off and dresses me in a girl's bikini. I act like a girl and he acts like my boyfriend. I pretend I'm a virgin and don't know anything about sex. He tries to seduce me and says things like "I'll show you mine if you'll show me yours," "If I show you mine, will you kiss it?" and "If you let me see it, I'll kiss it." We make this act drag out for hours. Sometimes it gets us so excited that we both come, even though I still have my clothes on and he's still trying to get into my pants. He likes to pull the bottoms of the bikini to one side and fuck me while I'm still wearing them. I jerk myself off when he does this. I do it to make him mad. He does not like me to waste perfectly good come like this. He likes it all for himself. Sometimes I come into a glass or something while he's fucking me. When he's through with my ass, he scoops the come out with his fingers and eats it that way. He says it gives him something to do with his hands when I'm in his ass.

Once he was fucking me and telling me not to jerk off, but I did anyway. When he was through, he pretended to be mad. He chained me to a tree for being naughty. He said if I'd suck him off, he'd forgive me and turn me loose. I told him no and he whipped me. He didn't really hurt me. It's a game we play all the time. I pretend I'm in great pain and moan and groan a lot. Finally I tell him I can't stand it anymore. I will do anything he wants if only he'll stop. Then he gets his blow job and I get a piece of his ass or whatever I want.

He's got a big old horse on the farm. We ride it what we call bareback. It really is bareback. The horse does not have a saddle. But the reason we call it bareback is that we're bare. He rides in front and I ride behind him with my hands on his stomach. My cock is shoved up inside him. It's a great feeling for both of us when the horse trots.

Sometimes he strokes the horse's cock until it gets an erection. He sucks the horse's cock while I suck his. He says the horse's semen tastes just like a man's except there's ten times more of it.

We do a lot of work with dildos and vibrators. I get him to kneel on the bed. I grease him up good and put the dildo in. It's a big long rubber thing shaped like a cock but much larger than a real cock. At first it's hard to get it into him. I take my time. I'm nice and gentle and slow and it takes time to get it in. It takes more time before I can get the whole thing in. I keep oiling him with mineral oil, and after a while he can take the whole thing. After he's got the whole thing up his ass, I start moving it in and out faster and faster, harder and harder. By the time he comes, I'm wringing wet with sweat from all the work. When he's rested up after his orgasm, he does the same thing for me. It's one of the finest orgasms there is because it takes so long to get to it. When you come with this one, you really come. It takes all the come out of you, every drop. If there's an orgasm better than this one, it's when there are three guys having sex. One guy's in his ass with the dildo slamming away, and I'm on my knees in front of him. Just before he shoots, he grabs my head and pulls me onto his cock. This way he's sure he doesn't have any come left. It's a nice feeling for me, too, because the dildo makes him come almost twice as much as usual. We did this one weekend after not having had any sex all week. The amount of come we gave each other was marvelous. We both gagged, but we got it all down. * * * *

I NEED DANGER AND PROBABLY HELP

This man is a doctor. The first thing he asked me was whether I was a therapist of some kind. He said he thinks he needs therapy, but he's afraid to seek it from his colleagues. He's afraid that if the word gets out about his fantasies and the behavior they lead him to, his practice will suffer. He's also afraid of ridicule. He claims to have never told anybody his fantasies before. He's curious how I will react. He's curious about my knowledge of psychiatry and analysis. Would I recognize mental illness if I saw it, he wants to know.

Homosexual Fantasies 89

* * * * I'm gay. I'm almost forty and I've never had a woman in my life. I must have examined 5,000 women in my practice, and never once have I been stimulated. I'm not repulsed either. I know many of my colleagues have a nurse present during female examinations as much to protect themselves from their patients and vice versa. I've never had the problem. The female body, to me, is a marvelously complex and wonderful machine that sometimes gets out of whack. I'm sort of like a skilled mechanic who locates the trouble, fixes it, presents his bill, and goes on to the next job.

I don't think being gay is a sickness. I was born that way. The way I am is the way God intended me to be. My preference is men who are straight. I look and act straight myself. Nobody except my sex partners knows or guesses that I'm gay. When I was younger, I used to go to the gay bars, find a nice-looking guy or guys, and take them home. I won't bore you with the physical details. With my partners, my behavior is normal gay. No sado-masochism or anything else freaky. Just oral and anal sex.

I like really masculine guys. Guys with mustaches or beards. Cops, truck drivers, construction workers, big married straight guys with dozens of children. Whenever I see a guy like this, I fantasize that he is fucking me or I am going down on him. I regard this as harmless. It gives me a thrill to make mental pictures like this. At night when the office is closed and I'm free until the next day, I search for partners. I go to straight bars and clubs and pick men up in the men's room. I have a regular routine. I go into the john. If there's a man there, I ask him if he'd like to have his cock sucked. If he says yes, I suck him off right there.

This is the behavior I'm worried about. For the past several months I have been putting myself in situations where the likelihood of my being caught is high. And I'm also blowing guys who are complete and absolute strangers. This is not safe because many men turn mean after a blow job. Their guilts over having another man bring them to orgasm raises fears in them about their own masculinity. They translate their fears into hostility. I've been getting into fights recently.

There are movie houses all over this town whose men's rooms are famous throughout the gay world. You can find action there. You walk in and as many men are having sex as those using the toilets. Heterosexuals who like to beat up on gays go to these places. And so do the cops. If they have a slow night, they go to these johns and bust everybody in sight. Knowing this, I go to these johns several times a month. The cops picked me up once. They caught me absolutely red-handed and in the act. They turned me loose when they found out I was a doctor.

My fantasies recently revolve around having sex with men in semipublic places and getting caught with a cock in my mouth or up my ass. I see myself blowing guys in johns, phone booths, in a darkened theatre, in doorways, in construction shacks. I'm blowing strangers, and while I'm sucking, I'm wondering if they'll turn mean after I've brought them off. Sometimes they do and sometimes they don't. I enjoy it both ways.

One fantasy I've been having recently is that I invite a whole group of strangers to my house. I suck them all off, let them all fuck me, and then they all turn mean. They really kick the shit out of me. Almost all the fantasies I have, I act out. I haven't actually done this one yet, but I want to, and knowing me, I probably will. Well, I'm a kind of nice-looking man. If I start doing this kind of thing, I'm going to start looking like a prizefighter, and what's worse, I'll probably get my hands busted up. Surgeons with broken hands don't get to heal very many sick people.

I've read around in the literature enough to know that everybody has sexual fantasies. So there's nothing wrong there. But how about this need for danger that's been cropping up? Do I want to lose my practice? Do I want pain inflicted on me? Years ago, I got involved in an S and M thing. I didn't like it at all. I'm still not interested. At least I'm not interested in whips and spurs and the other paraphernalia that one traditionally associates with S and M. What apparently I am unconsciously looking for is the complete ruination of my life.

Does this sound sick, or does it sound like overdramatizing? In either case, it sounds like I at least should go to talk to a shrink. What do you think? * * * *

I gave this troubled doctor the names and telephone numbers of two psychiatrists in this city and recommended that he apply for treatment. He didn't call them.

GRAND CENTRAL STATION

* * * * I'm seventeen and will graduate from high school this year. I'm gay. What I'm going to tell you about are things I've actually done. But they're fantasies, too, because I think about them when I'm masturbating. I masturbate every day at least once. I think masturbating is good for you. It makes it easy for me to go to sleep. Just before I go to bed, I go into the bathroom and brush my teeth, and then I masturbate into the toilet and think about my fantasies while I do it. Sometimes I masturbate in bed and come into my own mouth. My come tastes like everybody else's. I wish I could suck my own cock. I've tried to for years. The closest I can get is three or four inches away from my mouth. I can't even lick it. Also, sometimes I masturbate in the morning before I piss. I always wake up with a hard on.

I think about other men when I masturbate, sometimes one man, and sometimes whole groups of them. Sometimes one man is fucking me up the ass while I fuck somebody else up the ass while I'm sucking another one off. I am holding cocks in each of my hands, masturbating them. The guy I'm sucking comes first. Then the two guys I'm jerking off come into my mouth. Another guy gets into my mouth. The guy in my ass comes, which makes me come. The guy I'm fucking, I'm also jerking off, and the guy I'm sucking has his mouth on the head of his (the one I'm jerking off) cock. The new guy comes in my mouth, and the one I'm jerking off comes at the same time.

Well, no. I've never really had it this good really. But I sure do think about it a lot. What has happened in real life is me fucking one guy while another fucks me. Boy, that was good. I think about doing it again, but I don't know how to find those two guys. Thinking about a cock up my ass is sometimes better than actually having one up there. Sometimes men get carried away while they're fucking me, and they hurt me and make me bleed. That never happens in fantasy.

I like to go to public bathrooms and watch men piss. They see me watching them, and they know I'm gay and that I want to suck them. Sometimes they let me. Grand Central Station is the best place for this. The men's bathroom is downstairs and off in a corner and kind of inconvenient to get to. So it's seldom very crowded. You can get some privacy there. I don't need privacy myself. I like it when men watch me suck, and I like to watch other people do it. But most men don't like other people watching while I suck. When a guy decides he'd like me to suck him, we go into one of the stalls. He either sits on the john and I kneel in front of him, or he stands on the seat, bending way over so people can't see his head and shoulders and I stand up and suck him that way. All other people can see is my feet, and they think I'm pissing.

I like the kneeling way, myself. In the first place, it's a thrill to kneel in front of a man. I feel like a page kneeling in front of his king or a slave in front of his master. But the reason I like to kneel most in Grand Central is that when people see me, they know perfectly well what I'm doing. Some men are turned on by what they see, and when I finish off the man I'm sucking, another man will be waiting outside to come in.

One of my best fantasies is that there's a long line of guys waiting to get off in my mouth. Do you suck cock? Well, when you suck a guy off, it's like you're getting some of his strength and masculinity into yourself. After I've sucked a guy off, I really feel great, you know? And after I've sucked off two guys, I feel twice as good. So I think about sucking off a whole line of guys, fifty or more. When I've blown the last one, I'm feeling like a superman or something. I feel very strong and masculine. I've talked with some of my friends about this. Sucking guys off makes them feel the same way. Of course the fantasy about sucking off fifty guys, one after the other, can't happen. I sucked off three guys once, one after the other. At the end of the third guy, my jaw muscles were so tired, I couldn't handle a fourth.

Boy, talking to you about this has really turned me on. I've got a big hard on. Would you like me to suck you off? Do you live anywhere near Grand Central? I live just a few blocks from there. I can come to your place, or if you live near the station, I can meet you in the men's room. Have you ever had a blow job?

I went to Grand Central one day last week. Before I started looking for guys to suck, I took a leak. While I was pissing, the man in the next urinal started staring at my cock. I could feel his eyes on it. After I was through pissing, I started playing with myself a little bit. I looked at him in the eyes and he looked back. He told me I was a beautiful boy and that he would like to suck my cock. I told him I would really like to let him. We left the bathroom and went into a room that had a whole bunch of electrical gear in it. He had a key for the door. We went in. He put his briefcase on the floor and knelt on it to keep from getting his pants dirty. That was really a very experienced guy. He really knew how to make a cock happy. He sucked very hard and kept moving his tongue back and forth at the same time. I came in nothing flat. He got up, and I knelt down in front of him and started undoing his fly. He looked at his watch and said he had to catch a train. I hated to lose his come. He was a nice man and I really wanted to suck him off a lot. I really want to suck you off a lot.

In the summertime I go to Bryant Park in back of the Forty-second Street library. On a nice night the place is crawling with gays. The whole city knows about this, and guys who want blow jobs come there. If you like to suck cock, it's a great place to go. But there are dangers in Bryant Park. Guys who like to beat up on gays also go there. I've been lucky so far. Whenever I go there, I find two or three guys to blow, but some of my friends have had some pretty bad times.

Sometimes when I masturbate I think about what happened in the park one night last summer. What you do to pick up guys in the park is this: You sit on a bench under a light. If you see a good-looking guy whose . . .

I forgot to tell you something. Remember when I was telling you how good I feel after sucking a guy off? Remember I said it makes me feel strong and masculine after I've done it? Well, I forgot to tell you that sucking off a straight guy is twice as good as blowing a gay. When I swallow a gay guy's come, I really feel fine. No complaints. But when I get a straight guy's come in my mouth, that's really something. It's like an injection of rocket power or something. When you can get that kind of come, the come of a real man, you become a real man yourself. I don't think straights get as much sex as gays because all the straights

I've sucked off have about twice as much come as gays. That means they've been saving it up, not having any sex. So not only do I get more powerful come when I blow a straight, I get more of it. I'm sure you're going to say no, but you'd really be doing me a big favor if you'd let me blow you. I like your voice. I'll bet your cock is huge. Look, you're a normal man. You like orgasms, right? So I'll give you a sensational orgasm. That's good for you. I'll get some super, number one, Grade A come for myself, and that's good for me. What do you say? What was I telling you before? Oh, yeah.

So if a guy is walking toward you and you like his looks and want him in your mouth, you stare at his fly and smile or lick your lips or do something to let him know what's on your mind. They usually sit down and you talk for a few minutes, and then you ask him if he'd like you to suck his cock. The answer is always yes. So you go off in the bushes and blow him. You kneel on a newspaper, by the way, to keep from getting your pants dirty.

Well, I was sitting on a bench this one night last summer when this dynamite-looking guy comes along. He's got on tight pants, and I can tell by the big, sexy-looking bulge that this is my kind of cock coming at me. I look at his fly and smile and lick my lips, but the guy is reading a newspaper while he's walking and he doesn't see me. He walks up to my bench and walks right on by. What am I going to do? I want that guy's cock in my mouth so much I can taste it already.

If a guy comes up to you in Bryant Park, it's okay to ask him if he'd like you to blow him. The cops used to try to trap you into making a play for them, but the courts have started calling that entrapment and throwing the cases out. So the cops don't try to get you to make an offer after they start talking to you. What they do nowadays is try to make you come to them. If you approach a cop first and ask him to let you blow him, you've committed a crime. It's called indecent something, I think.

Well, anyhow, this guy with the big bulge is just too good for me to let get away. I run after him. When I catch up to him, I tell him the truth. I tell him that bulge in his pants as he walked by has got me all hot and bothered. If he has a little time, I'd really like to suck him off.

He smiles at me and we go off into the bushes. I get down on my knees and he takes this thing out that looks like it belongs on a horse. I mean that cock is just gigantic. When he first pulled it out, he had about half a hard on. When I reach out and touch it and kiss it a couple of times, it starts to come up to full size. In a second or so, I'm kneeling at the feet of the man of every faggot's dream. Big, heavy, throbbing up and down.

I get the thing in my mouth with some trouble and lean into him. I want all of this I can get in my mouth and down my throat. When he gets to the back of my throat, I can't get it down. I've never in my life found one I can't sword-swallow, but this thing is just too big. I push into him hard trying to swallow and he starts coming. He hasn't been in my mouth yet for half a minute and here he comes. He got excited and grabbed my head and pulled me into him. He was a very strong guy and he pulled me into him hard enough so that down my throat she goes, coming every inch of the way. The way he came, he could not have gotten laid for a year. I suck and suck and suck, and he comes and comes and comes. And while I'm sucking, I'm thinking one time is not enough. I want this one again. When he's finished coming, his cock does not go down. It got a little softer, but it stayed just as big. I slowly back away from him and, inch by inch, he comes out, and I hear somebody whistle and say, "Jesus H. Christ." We both jump and look around, and there's a cop standing there not two feet from us. He's looking at my man's enormous cock and shaking his head from side to side. He's never seen anything this big either. My man quickly stuffs it back in his pants, and I get on my feet, watching him. I am going to get busted, my parents will find out I'm gay, they'll have to pay a fine, I may go to a detention home, and the whole thing, and I'm not thinking of any of those things. I'm watching him try to stuff that monster in his pants. All I want to do is watch. The cop is watching him, too. When he finally gets the job done, the cop says something like: "Sorry, boys. You'll have to come with me." And superstud reaches into his pocket, pulls out his wallet, and shows the cop his badge and ID.

Superstud is a cop!

The two guys talk for a couple of minutes, and I know everything will be all right. My man comes over to me and tells me everything is okay. And then he asks me if I will blow him again. He says the cop, the other cop, would like to see how a little guy like me can get a whang like that down. This is like asking me if I'll take a million dollars or something. Down I go on my knees again. I open up his fly for him and pull it out of him, and in a second or so, there it is again, the Monster of Bryant Park. The other cop just can't believe its size. I get it into my mouth and start sucking. I suck and lick and lean into him, and right down my throat it goes. No trouble this time. I get it all the way down until my nose is flattened up against his hair. Back and forth I go, getting it all down when I go forward and sucking on the head when I move back. I got to suck him for maybe ten minutes before he came. It was as good the second time as it was the first. But there was so much of it, I lost some. I missed it, but not much, because what he had was plenty. When I let him out of my mouth, he was limp. But the other cop wasn't. He'd gotten turned on watching me work. I hope he didn't want me to suck him off. My jaws ached. I was tired and out of breath. My mouth was all stretched out of shape. My man put his cock in his pants and zipped up. He said goodnight to us and left.

The other cop came over and stood in front of me. He took his cock out and I took it in my mouth. I liked it. It was a nice, big, normal cock with a lot of taste to it. I think he'd been with a woman. I gave him a good blow job, and he gave me a nice, big mouthful of come. I told him I hoped he didn't want it again. He said no, he had to save some for his wife when he got off duty. He told me to stay out of the park, but he didn't say it like he meant it. He asked me if I'd ever seen anything like the first cop. I told him never and went home. I did some jerking off that night before I went to sleep. I'm masturbating now as I remember. That was my best night ever. * * * *

PHOTOGRAPHS

* * * * I'm white but I really dig black guys. I'll take a white guy or a woman now and then, but black guys are the best. I let them pick

me up in bars. I prefer two at once. You get more sex that way, and everybody gets a chance to build up more come while taking the pictures.

When we get to the black guy's apartment, he strips and I blow him. I blow him after I have sucked his nipples for a while and carried him around the apartment on my shoulders with his cock in my mouth. I don't suck him then. I just hold his cock in my mouth and get it big for him. When I'm through blowing him, I lick him all over, spending most of the time on his asshole. This lubricates it and excites him so I can fuck him in the ass if I want to, or I can blow him again. Sometimes both. Is your book going to have pictures? I have hundreds of them. Well, do you want the pictures anyhow? They're free. Well, if you don't want them, can you give me the names of people who do? I have pictures of me with women, too. I have a whole series of me fucking one woman while I'm eating another, and I have plenty of me eating one woman while another is blowing me. White chicks and black. Do you want to see these? Say, doesn't anything turn you on? * * * *

3

BISEXUAL FANTASIES

MARRIED AND BISEXUAL

* * * * I was an officer in the Navy during World War II and was stationed in Hawaii, assigned to duty in the officer's club. I had never had a homosexual experience. A new recruit arrived one day, and I knew my first experience was coming up. He was eighteen years old and beautiful. He had dark hair and brown eyes and a finely proportioned body. His mouth was full and sensuous. He was a typical eighteen-year-old American boy. He had a girl friend back home, an abhorrence of homosexuality, and he was timid about heterosexual contacts, too.

One day, while on duty early in the morning, I passed by his bunk while he lay sleeping. His penis was hanging out of his skivvies. The sight of it made an indelible impression. I can see it as clearly today as I saw it then.

I returned from liberty late one night when all hands slept except C.J.H. I feigned drunkenness and lured him into the admiral's quarters, a room set aside in the club for visiting VIPs. I plied him with liquor and told him how hard up I was. I told him I was used to getting laid a couple of times a week and that I was really horny. I had gone to town to fuck my girl, and she had turned me down. She was menstruating. (I didn't have a girl.)

He was envious of me because I had seen sea duty and he had not. I told him stories of sex at sea. I told him about a game called firing line. The men lined up against a bulkhead and masturbated. The man who shot farthest collected the kitty, five dollars each from the other men. Another game I told him about was the matching game. Two men thrust their erect penises at each other. The man whose penis first touched the other's belly won and would be masturbated by the loser.

By this time in my narrative, C.J.H. is pretty horny and drunk. He lets me fondle him and perform fellatio on him.

I am forty-nine, married, and bisexual. * * * *

I'M VERY MUCH INTO MYSELF

Here are the fantasies of two men, friends, who called me separately. The first man, Don, is bisexual. Frank considers himself heterosexual although he and Don frequently have sex together for the amusement of their friends.

* * * * I married this damn kewpie doll of a wife. She was one of those damn gigglers, you know? So I dumped her. I can suck my own cock, so who needs her, right? I'm into gymnastics. I work the bars and rings. Every now and then I show the guys at the gym how supple I am. I blow myself, and it really turns them on. After I blow myself, I blow them and some of them blow me. I get invited to a lot of orgies. People like to have me at orgies because I turn people on, and the party gets started much quicker after I blow myself.

Hello, Bill, I'm Frank, a friend of Don's. He tells me you're a nice guy and easy to talk to. He said I should call you on the phone and tell you what we do together. The first thing you should know is that from my collarbone to my knees, I'm tattooed all over. Every inch of me is tattooed, including my cock. I have this snake that comes out of my ass, around my belly, down into the pubic hairs, and out onto my cock. The snake is all green and red and yellow. Every scale on him is perfect.

At parties, people always ask me to take off my clothes so they can see the artwork. I usually oblige, particularly if I'm horny. My snake really turns girls on. A lot of them take one look and either drag me into the nearest bedroom or go down on me right there on the spot.

I was at an orgy one time and I saw Don suck himself off. I'd had some drinks and was feeling kind of playful. Did he tell you how he does it? Well, he lies on his back with his ass in the air. Then he lowers his joint into his mouth. Get the picture? Okay. So I see him at this party this night and while his ass is in the air, I butter up the snake and slip it into his ass. It just cracked everybody up. So Don and I go to orgies together and are now getting paid for it. Listen, you're a writer, right? Do you know anybody at *Playgirl* or *Penthouse?* I think they might be interested in having Don and me do our thing for their centerfold. How much do they pay models, do you happen to know?

Say, Don's right. You're a real nice guy. Would you like me and Don to come over and show you our act? What do you think the chances are that *Playboy* would buy pictures of girls going down on my snake or me putting it to some chick? Think Hefner would go for that?
* * * *

HOLY AND FORBIDDEN SEX

This man is a barber and a hair stylist. He's thirty, bisexual, and has a college degree. He told me where he worked. Because it was just a few blocks from my office, after he finished telling me his fantasies I walked to his shop. All the barbers were women. I assume that what this man told me was also purest fantasy.

* * * * When I was a kid about fourteen, I had a teacher, a Mr. Waters. He was very handsome. I used to watch him walking back and forth in front of the class writing things on the blackboard. Sometimes

I'd see him from the front and sometimes from the back. I didn't learn very much in his class because, as soon as he came in the room, I mentally took his clothes off. In my mind's eye, I pictured his penis as huge and circumcised so I could get a good look at the head of his cock. When he walked back and forth, his penis and balls bounced and swung.

When Mr. Waters asked me a question, his penis would be pointing right at me. Whenever he spoke to me, he got a hard on. In my fantasy, of course. I used to picture myself going up to the front of the class and kneeling in front of him and sucking him off in front of everybody. I dreamed that I sucked cock so well, that if I could get his cock in my mouth, he wouldn't want to pull it out even though everybody was watching. Sometimes I pictured him putting me over his desk and fucking me in the ass. When he was through, he'd suck me off and let me fuck him in the ass.

Most of these daydreams came true. He kept me after class a couple of times. I think he was trying to screw up his courage to ask me something. Finally, he popped the question. "I've noticed," he said, "that when I walk back and forth in front of the class that you're always following me with your eyes. And your eyes are always glued to my crotch. Is there anything you want to tell me?"

I told him my fantasies. Mr. Waters was handsome, as I've said, and he was also gay. Before him, I had never had a man, or a woman for that matter. He was a great teacher outside the classroom, too. I went to his rooms almost every day for the rest of the school year. He was very skilled and gentle. His cock in real life, as in my fantasies, was huge and circumcised. But despite its size, he never hurt me with it, not even the first time he fucked me. Not only did he not hurt me, he made it sensational for me. While he fucked me, he jerked me off. When he came inside me, the feeling was so great I came too.

Today, I still fantasize about Mr. Waters. He's about the best I ever had. And today I fantasize other things, too. I see myself fucking nuns and priests. I see them fucking each other and fucking and sucking me. I see myself fucking them in church on the altar. I have this great picture fucking a priest beneath his robes while he's saying mass.

I'm finger-fucking one of the altar boys, while at the same time I'm running a crucifix in and out of a nun's cunt. All of us are having a fine time.

The congregation is filled with old people. I mean really old people. Up in their eighties and older. They watch us cavort on the altar. They get turned on watching us. Some of them beg us to come fuck and suck them. Soon everybody in the church is doing everybody else. I love those wrinkled, clean, old cocks that haven't been hard in years. The look of happiness on everybody's face is beautiful. The nuns are the happiest of all. They're lying on their backs with their black robes up and their white panties down. They masturbate themselves with crucifixes. They stuff their beads up their asses. At the moment of orgasm, they pull the beads out and scream because it feels so good. Some of the nuns fuck each other with crucifixes.

I like having these fantasies in church. I take the priest's clothes off, just like Mr. Waters. I watch his penis swing. I go up and suck it while he says the mass.

None of this happens in real life. I have sex with men and women my own age. I've never had a nun or a priest. But if the opportunity ever comes up, I'll jump at it. Just thinking about it has really turned me on. How old are you? Can I come suck you off? Will you come over here? I guarantee the best blow job you ever had. Well, here's my telephone number in case you change your mind. * * * *

After finding out that this man fantasized his occupation or at least his place of business, I called the number he gave me. It was out of service.

JACK THE RAPER

The man who telephoned the following fantasy terminated the call twice and moaned and grunted throughout. In all the previous fantasies, I have edited and rearranged the calls and interviews to make them coherent stories. This time I'm reporting the call verbatim.

* * * * Hello, Mr. Price, I'm calling about your article in *Screw*.

Well, I'm thirty-two and have a high school. I'm single and straight. I fantasize I am sucking off little boys' penises. I am five years old. I take the whole penis in my mouth. I feel their asses [he's breathing hard and moaning now]. I stick my penis . . . but I can't. Also I get them to suck my penis and they come in my mouth. I want to suck all the beautiful asses of all the little boys. I think about fucking women up the ass. I can suck my own penis. I do rape women and fuck them up the ass. [Long, loud groan at this point and he hangs up. Few minutes later, he's on the phone again, out of breath.]

Hello, Mr. Price, it's me again. I used to do . . . I used to deliver food in Queens. I delivered by bike. I lived at home. I made a delivery to this woman right around where I live. She was about forty. Supermarket delivery boy. I brought the package in. Helping her take the stuff into the kitchen. She bent down to do something. Short skirt. Such a beautiful ass. [He's moaning a little now.] So I got right in back of her and pulled her panties down and put my hand over her mouth. I stuck my penis up her ass. I fucked her in the ass. I came. Then when I was finished fucking her in the ass, I took my hand off her mouth and came in her mouth. When I was finished with that, I ate her. After that she didn't care very much. * * * *

What was so upsetting about this call is that I didn't think it was fantasy. In retrospect, I suspect it is. Would he rape a woman in his own neighborhood? Wouldn't she report him? If he actually raped one woman, quite likely he raped others under the same circumstances. Wouldn't anybody report him?

ALL IN THE FAMILY

* * * * This all happened years ago when I was a child. I remember it in all its vivid detail and the remembering is fine. I was eighteen years old. I had been to New York City a day or so before. I had bought an illustrated sex manual. My mother had caught me reading it and had taken it away.

I was lying in bed that night, playing with myself and thinking about the teacher at school I had been fucking and thinking about Dick. I wished that either of them were in bed with me. I thought about a threesome and all the wonderful combinations. My cock was really big. In real life it's so big that, when it's erect, I can't close my fingers around it.

I wasn't really masturbating, I was just sort of playing with myself, when I heard a noise on the fire escape and saw a figure move stealthily by the window. I put on a bathrobe and went to the window and looked out. Someone was crouching in the darkness outside my parents' window. He was looking in.

I climbed out on the fire escape, not making any noise because I was not wearing shoes, and crept toward the Peeping Tom. In the dim light coming from the bedroom window, I recognized my sister, in bathrobe and nightgown, peering in. Her robe was parted and she had a hand up her nightgown.

I touched her shoulder and she jumped. She stood up and looked at me with terror in her eyes. She thought I was going to tell on her. I told her to go back to my room and wait for me. She was a year younger than me and did as she was told.

I looked through the window. My parents were naked. My father was lying across the arms of an overstuffed chair, reading my sex book. My mother was smearing a big, white, double dildo with KY Jelly. She spread my father's cheeks and smeared him with it. She put the dildo inside herself and put the other end of it in my father's ass. His cock, which had been hanging down limp, got erect. She held him on either side of his ass and slammed away at him like a man. Tears were streaming down his cheeks from the pain. My mother's face was distorted and her mouth was open and her hair was flying. My father shot off and dropped the book. My mother kept at it, faster and faster. My father did not lose his erection and was now jerking off. My mother came and fell off him, pulling the dildo out of him as she did. The dildo made a little sucking sound as it came out.

I stroked myself as I watched.

I went back to my room, my cock as hard as a rock, and climbed in through the window. Sally sat on my bed waiting for me. She looked up as I climbed in and saw my cock sticking through the front of the robe.

I asked her what she had been doing outside my parents' window. She said that she and her boyfriend had just started having sex and that neither one of them knew very much about it. They had decided to spy on their parents to find out.

I was standing in front of her, my cock just inches away from her head. She glanced at it every now and then while she talked to me. She said it was much bigger than her boyfriend's. I raised her up to me and kissed her. I forced her mouth open with my tongue and explored the inside of it. My cock was throbbing on our bellies. She began sucking on my lips and tongue. I took off her robe and let it fall to the floor. I opened my robe, let it fall, and pulled her nightgown over her head. I laid her down on the bed and began sucking her tits and playing with her cunt. I put her hand on my cock. At first she just let it rest there, but in a minute or so, she was stroking it back and forth.

I knelt beside her head and told her to kiss it. She said no. She was looking at the little drop of moisture that had just appeared. I put my hands in her hair and pulled her to me. She did not resist. She kissed it. I told her to lick it. She licked my moisture off her lips and began licking me. I tried to force it into her mouth, but she would not take it. I told her to take it in her mouth and suck on it. She said she had never done that before and didn't think she ought to. I told her I had done it a thousand times with Dick and it was fun to do.

She put the head in her mouth and started sucking. She gave it about three good sucks, and I started coming. She tried to get it out of her mouth, but I held her hard by the ears. She had to eat all of it; her mouth was stretched so tight by my size that she had no choice. I took it out of her mouth. She held my balls, kneading them and staring at my cock.

"I liked it," she said. Then she took me in her mouth again until I got hard. I spread her legs and put it inside her and fucked her till we both came.

After that, she came to my room every night, until I got drafted. She's married now, but I still fuck her every chance I get. Once her husband got drunk and passed out, and she blew me in the same room with him while playing with his cock.

After I fucked her, I rolled off to get my strength back and saw that my door was open and Timmy, my thirteen-year-old brother, was standing in the door way. He said he had heard noises that sounded as if someone was getting hurt. He had come to investigate. I asked what he had seen. He said he'd seen me fucking.

He came over to the bed. His cock was making his pajamas bulge. I undid the button and out it popped. It was as big as mine. I took it in my mouth and began sucking on it. Sally said she wanted to do it. I told her we could both do it. I'd suck till he came, and then I'd switch his cock into her mouth and she could get the rest of it. After we both had had his come, she said she wanted him to fuck her, too. He climbed on her and started pumping away and I went to the bathroom for hair tonic.

I rubbed my cock with it and Timmy's ass and asshole. I put a finger into him, then two, and finally three. As gently as I could, I eased into him. It took us a few minutes to get our rhythms right, but when we got the rhythm smooth, it was a great way to fuck. It was particularly good for Sally who had orgasm after orgasm. Timmy never came to my room again after this, but Sally would let him come to her room sometimes, when we were through. After we were through on the first night, she asked us to fuck her up the ass. We were both too tired. The next night, after she'd blown me, I fucked her in the ass. She loved that, too. And still does. * * * *

SEX WITH A GALLIC FLAVOR

* * * * I am forty-four, divorced, a foreigner, and very lonely. My accent accounts for the loneliness. I speak and people don't understand. My sex is mostly masturbation. I lie on my bed and masturbate and come into a towel. When I masturbate I think about things that I have done or wished I had done. These things I think about to make my cock hard are fantasies.

I was born and raised on a farm in France. When I was a little boy, my sisters and my two brothers used to masturbate a friend of mine. Then my oldest brother would masturbate me. We used to do this almost every day. My sisters were fascinated with our penises. They laughed. They laughed when we first took our penises out because they were so small. They laughed when we started to manipulate ourselves and each other. When the penises started to grow, they laughed most. My oldest brother was the only one old enough to come, to squirt sperm. He was sort of the hero and he knew it. When the rest of us came, nothing happened that one could see. But when my brother came, everybody could see what was happening. The white sperm shot out. My friend, my other brother, and I were envious because my sisters liked to watch my older brother and not us. They liked to watch all of us until my brother would say, "Watch! Watch! Watch! Watch!" He would say this in time to his strokings.

We knew that what we were doing was wrong because we hid from our parents. I think the fact that it was wrong was what made it such fun.

In the beginning, only the boys masturbated. The girls never touched us or themselves. My older sister one day touched our brother's sperm. Usually he shot into the air and the sperm would fly out and fall into the straw. But one day the sperm landed on a wall. My older sister went to the wall to look at it. She touched it with her finger and smelled her finger. She said it smelled very good. Always after this my brother always put his sperm on places where we could touch it and smell it. Once after I had touched it, I tasted my finger. His sperm tasted as good as it smelled. Everybody else, after I had done this, tasted their fingers and liked the taste.

One day we were masturbating and the girls were watching. The girls began touching themselves. I guess they had talked it over and decided to show us that they masturbated, too. They did not push and pull back and forth as the boys did. They rubbed their dresses up and down. My brother wanted to see more, but they would not lift their dresses and lower their pants. Later they did. My older sister had a little hair. She put her finger inside herself and made a circular motion with it. The younger sister just rubbed herself with one finger while holding herself open with two other fingers. The girls stood when they did this, and the boys knelt close to them so we could see what they did. While they did this, we masturbated. We watched the girls and they watched us. It was very good. We smelled and tasted their fingers when they were through. The smell and taste were much different from my brother's. But we thought it was very good. My brother licked my big sister's pussy. She almost fell down. She said it felt so good her knees became weak. My brother said he liked the taste. Both my sisters let all the boys taste them, and they tasted each other. Everybody liked the taste. After this, our sisters masturbated in front of us always, and they always let us lick them and put our tongues inside them. The boys masturbated when we did this, and we started making them come this way.

My cock is very hard as I am talking to you. I am rubbing it and remembering the good times we boys and girls had. I hope you don't mind. Are you hard, too?

When I went to bed at night, I used to think about what we all did together during the day, and I used to masturbate until I went to sleep. I think the girls did the same thing and talked about what we were all doing because, one day, instead of the boys kneeling and licking the girls, they knelt in front of my friend and my brother and licked them. I masturbated while I watched. My brother started saying "Watch! Watch!" We thought my sister would stop licking, but she did not. His sperm went on her nose and mouth and chin. Some of it went in her mouth and she swallowed it. His cock was limp. She put it in her mouth and began sucking it. He became stiff. When he came, she swallowed it while the rest of us watched and masturbated. From this time on until we grew up and moved away, our sisters would suck us every day and we would lick them until they came. I return to France every three or four years. When I see my sisters, if their husbands and children are not present, we do sixty-nine. Both my sisters like anal sex with me now, too. We do not think we are doing incest because neither my brother nor I ever put our penises in their vaginas.

My friend and I used to masturbate each other and suck each other off when my sisters and brothers were not there. Once, after watching a male sheep mount a female, we mounted her when she was finished. It was good. Later that day my sister began to suck me. She took my penis out of her mouth and spat. She said she would not do it any more until I had washed myself.

One day shortly after I came to this country, I was waiting on a table occupied by a young French couple. They had been here a short time, too. We liked each other. They gave me their address and told me to come for a drink when I was through work. I went to their apartment. I don't think any of us thought about having sex, but it happened. The woman, after a lot of wine, was sitting in a way that I could see up her dress. My cock got hard and both of them could see it. She asked if I would show it to them. I pulled it out and her husband got hard, too. I asked her husband if he would allow me to see his wife. He told her that if she wished me to see her, he gave his permission. She took her pants down and sat in the chair again and pulled up her knees. She pulled her vagina open with her fingers so that her husband and I could see her. I asked if I could see her naked all over. She took her clothes off, and so did her husband and I. We looked at each other and touched each other. She turned around and spread her cheeks while bending over so we could look at her anus. I touched her there. She moved so that my finger went inside her. It was the softest, most pliant anus I had ever touched.

She told us she would like to play a game with us. She left the room and came back with a stop watch. She told us that she was going to suck us both. After that, she said she wanted both of us to fuck her at the same time. She said the one who took the longest to come in her mouth got his choice of fucking her in the anus or the pussy. She sucked her husband first. While she sucked him, he sucked one of her fingers to make it wet. She put that finger up his ass while she sucked. Her husband wanted to stay in her mouth the longest so he did things to distract himself. He asked me to bring him some wine. We talked and drank wine while she sucked and pushed her finger into him. I don't remember how long it took him to come, but it was a long time.

Just watching the two of them, I knew that the second her mouth touched my penis, I would come. I had not masturbated for several days. I was very ready for a big come. I know that when I am drunk I can keep myself from coming for a very long time. While she sucked him I drank three or four glasses of wine. I drank more wine as she sucked me. I lasted much longer than her husband. I lasted so long that I thought her mouth would become tired, but it did not become tired. I told her husband that I never knew a woman could suck a man for so long without resting. He told me that once she sucked ten men in one evening, one right after the other. When they got home that night, she sucked him again and went to sleep with his penis in her mouth. She sucked him twice the next morning without taking his penis out of her mouth for a rest.

I finally came. She congratulated me for lasting so long and lay down on the floor on her side. I wanted the back. I put my penis in her anus and her husband put his in her vagina. This was no good for me. I could not get inside her as deeply as I wanted. I asked her to bring us some pillows. I put the pillows on the floor underneath her husband's bottom. She squatted on top of him getting him inside her very deeply. I knelt behind her, between both their legs, and put my penis inside her. When I was in her as deeply as I thought I could get, she reached back and spread her cheeks apart and I went in even deeper. My penis could feel her husband's penis. In a few minutes, we found a rhythm that pleased us all. Because of all the wine we men had drunk, we stayed like this for a very long time. We gave her many orgasms before we had our first. We rested inside her for a few minutes and began again. The husband and I slept.

When I awoke, her husband was still sleeping. She was curled up in a chair. She was awake. She had two vibrators inside her. I told her I would go to the toilet and wash myself and come back and she could suck me if she wished. She followed me to the bathroom, the vibrators still inside her. She knelt in the bathtub and instructed me to urinate into her mouth. She did not swallow the urine. She let it fill her mouth and run out. As it ran down her chin, she caught it in her hands and rubbed it in her hair and over her body. We took a shower after this. I washed her and she washed me. Her husband came in then, and after he had urinated in her mouth, we both washed him. We returned to the living room. She took the vibrator from her anus and put it in him. She sucked him while I fucked her in the anus and the pussy. She switched the vibrator from place to place inside her to accommodate my desires. I asked if she had a vibrator for me. She said she did not. Her husband brought a candle, which he placed inside me and moved rapidly in and out of me while I fucked her and she sucked him. When we were through, I went home. They promised they would have another vibrator for me the next time I came.

I know a girl who likes to make love to me and her German shepherd at the same time. I fuck her in the front and the dog fucks her in the back. Or I fuck her and she sucks him. Or she sucks me while the dog fucks her.

I went to Florida on a short vacation recently. While there, I met a girl who liked me to hit her. She liked me to hit her and tell her to suck me. I would hit her and tell her to suck me, and she would say no. She liked me to continue hitting her until she sucked me. While she sucked me, she would masturbate herself with her fingers or cold bottles or vegetables from the refrigerator. Once, after she had masturbated herself with a large carrot, she asked me if I wanted to eat it. I ate it while she masturbated and watched me. Once we made love with ice cubes in our anuses. Once she had an ice cube in her anus and she asked me to shove it way up inside her with my penis. We both enjoyed this. She told me she was in Florida to get a divorce. She had discovered her husband making love to their nine-year-old daughter. She thought that was terrible.

A couple comes into the restaurant every now and then with their twenty-year-old son. Sometimes I visit them and we all make love together. All of us like both men and women. Sometimes there are their friends there, too. I don't like to see the son and father fucking and sucking each other. But if they enjoy it, I suppose it's all right.

I have talked to you a long time and have come on my towel many times during our conversation. Please permit me to give you the name and address of the restaurant where I work. Perhaps you and a friend would like to have me serve you a fine French meal. * * * *

I looked the restaurant up in the telephone book. It's there. I called it and he answered the phone. Which raises the question of how much of what he told me is invention and how much is recollective fantasy. It does seem to me that some of the positions he describes would be a touch intricate and uncomfortable. But if the Gallic zest for lust is as reputed, perhaps indeed all that he described took place. It also seems to me that this man might consider giving up waiting on tables and begin writing porn, which pays better, or directing porno flicks. With his sharp eye for detail, he'd be good at it.

WITH APOLOGIES TO MACDONALD

Many years ago, John D. MacDonald, the very good and mysteriously underrated writer, wrote a story called "The Girl, the Gold Watch and Everything." Among other daring items in the plot is the concept of stopping time. It's an old idea, of course, but not too often used because it's so difficult to deal with. It's virtually impossible to make the idea work in a story because of the credibility problem: Nobody really believes time can be stopped. MacDonald makes you believe.

The only thing I know about the man who phoned in the following is that he is not John D. MacDonald.

* * * * I'm sitting in a darkened theater. The play is in progress. I don't know what the play is about, but it's damned dull, and I have been daydreaming. I see myself riding a horse and jerking off. Or, there are three of us on the horse. Three guys. I'm in the middle. Guy behind me is fucking me in the ass. Guy in front is fucking me in the cunt. I'm a guy and don't have a cunt, but what the hell. It's only a fantasy.

Not only is the play dull, but the fantasies are, too.

I'm with a date, and he seems to be enjoying the play, so I just can't walk out. It's too dark to read the program notes. I can't sleep because I have a sinus problem and snore. So I cast around for a fantasy complex enough to last the hour or so the play will run. I toy with the idea of climbing up on the stage and fucking the leading lady, a real knockout. I reject the idea as too tame. And then it occurs to me to fuck everybody in the entire theater. Obviously, it can't be done. Before I finish with the first fuck, some damn prude would have called the police. Then I'd really be fucked. There must be some way.

I snap my fingers and time stops throughout the entire theater. It doesn't stop for me of course. I'm now sitting in a theater filled with motionless people. Only I am able to move.

I have always believed in working one's way up and saving the best for last. So I go downstairs and bugger the men's room attendant. I walk across the hall and piss on the lady in the lady's room. I go to the main floor and, one by one, carry the female ushers up to the stage. I undress them and put them in various sexual positions with the cast, who I also undress.

I undress the entire audience and hide their clothes in wardrobes. I drape their arms about each other, put penises in mouths and ears and asses and noses, put couples of the same and different sexes in the sixty-nine position.

A well-known rabbi is in the audience. I leave the theater and buy a glass of milk, a shrimp cocktail, and a ham sandwich and put them in his hands. Cardinal Cooke is in the audience. I kneel him in front of the rabbi and put the rabbi's cock in his mouth.

Then I call the city desk at the *New York Times.*

Before the reporters arrive, I whip up on stage and give gorgeous, the leading lady, a great fuck. Ass, mouth, and cunt.

I survey my handiwork. Beautiful. Like a Roman orgy but bigger and better.

I leave the theater and go to Sardi's and wait for the first edition of the *Times.* * * * *

Seems to me he should have called the *Daily News.* It's much more their kind of story.

BABY DOLL

* * * * I'm twenty-seven, single, bisexual, and a graduate student. I have many fantasies, both male and female. That is, I have fantasies in which I see myself as both male and female. I also have a fantasy in which I picture myself as a baby. I find this so appealing that

I act it out about once a month with a domineering partner. The partner can be either male or female.

My partner in the fantasy plays either my mother or my father. I undress and lie down on a rubber sheet. My mother, let's say, starts putting diapers on me. I am a baby and have no bladder control or control over my bowels. Sometimes when she is putting on the diaper, I let loose in one way or another, or sometimes both ways. She cleans me and powders me and gives me a bottle or lets me suckle her. If it's a male taking care of me, he gives me a pacifier several times a day. I'm sure you can imagine what this pacifier actually is.

I crawl around on the floor and occasionally break things. I am continually being told what to do and what not to do. When I break things or when I disobey, I am spanked and put in my crib. If I get caught playing with my penis, I get spanked. Sometimes, if I have both a father and a mother, they let me watch them make love. I am just a baby, so it doesn't matter if I see.

My fathers are all cruel and incestuous. Sometimes, when I'm crawling on the floor, they take my diapers off and spank me and put their penises in my ass. They know this is safe to do because I can't talk and tell on them. Sometimes they make me suck them off. Babies love to suck on things. I pretend that I am sucking a baby bottle and that their sperm is milk and is good for me. I'm one of those babies that is always hungry. Sometimes I suck off my father while my penis is inside my mother's mouth.

Because I am a baby, I don't know anything about sex. My mother and father are liberated in this area. They want me to find out how much fun sex can be. They teach me how to masturbate. They make me practice in front of them, sometimes for hours at a time, until I have no sperm left to shoot out. Sometimes they call in their friends and have me show them what I have learned. If my father and mother go out, the friends stay on as baby-sitters. They change me and powder me and sometimes clean me with their mouths. They masturbate in front of me and play with my genitals, masturbate me, make me suck them and masturbate them, and do other things baby-sitters do to children. If they catch me masturbating by myself, they tie my hands so I can't do it anymore. This always gives me an erection. They know I am thinking about sex, which is dirty, and they punish me by not letting me have anything to eat or drink, or they keep me in my crib, tied up for hours at a time, in the dark. When I get tired of this, I cry and carry on. When they figure I have had enough, or when my crying gets on their nerves, they come in and give me a bottle and hold me in their arms until the crying stops.

I hope writing you this has been helpful. My name is Kent. My telephone number is ―――――. If you would like to talk further about my fantasies, please call me. When I act these fantasies out, it's always with people I know well. It would be dangerous to do it with strangers, because, as a baby, I am completely at their mercy. However, because you're a writer, it would probably be safe to let you be my father. If you think you might enjoy it, please call me. Or if you think, in the interests of research, that you might like to spend a weekend with me, as an observer, please call. Most men never have the opportunity to have another human being completely at their mercy. I love being completely helpless and dependent on others to take care of me. If you would like to play with me like this, please call. I am too shy to call you. I would like a writer to take care of me. I have never met a writer before.
* * * *

ANDROGYNE

In biology, an androgyne is an organism that has within itself the characteristics of both sexes. An androgyne can breed with itself, alone, or with another androgyne. This man, a pre-med student, reports that he believes it is God's will for some men to be androgynous. His purpose here on earth, he believes, is to broaden men's sexual boundaries, to make them aware of what is possible sexually. As a medical student he knows he's not an androgyne. But when he fantasizes, he imagines he is one. In real life, he says, he has sex with both persuasions and has, on occasion, acted the part of a lesbian.

* * * * I am sexless. My penis has gone and so has my vagina.

Bisexual Fantasies 117

My two lovers, a man and a woman, look at me with disgust. They put me in the bathtub. They both straddle me and urinate on me to show their contempt. I am sorry I have disappointed them. My penis comes back, hard and strong. My vagina appears. The girl sucks me off in front while the man goes into my vagina from the rear. My tongue darts in and out of her cunt. She moans with pleasure. All three of us come at exactly the same instant. The girl's fluids flow into my mouth, the man's semen comes into me like an enema. The girl gags and chokes when I come, but she swallows it all anyhow.

She turns on the water and we carefully wash each other off. I taste the man's penis to see if it is clean. I taste the juices from my vagina. I lick and suck until he is clean. He comes again.

I am in a butch bar. All the women are burly and rough talking. A girl who looks as though she might be a truck driver is sitting alone drinking. I go over to her and introduce myself. I tell her I'm a doctor and I like her looks. She allows me to buy her a drink. Then she buys me one. I ask if she is free for the evening. She looks at me scornfully. I take her hand gently and put it between my legs. She is surprised and pleased that there is no penis there. We finish our drinks and go to my place. When she sees my fine vagina, she gets excited. She produces a dildo from her leather jacket pocket and sticks it into me. I suck furiously on her clitoris. The dildo is made of hard red rubber. It is about twice the thickness and length of a normal penis. It feels good inside me. I ask her if it's the kind that squirts warm cold cream. She tells me yes. When the time comes for me to come, I tell her to *Squeeze now.* She does and I am flooded. The cream smells perfumy and good, but I know it does not taste as good as semen.

My penis is very large. Again I am in a lesbian bar. The women look at me with contempt. Man-haters, all of them. What am I doing here? Why don't I leave? I take off my jacket and put it on the bar stool. I jump up and sit on the bar. I undo my fly and take my penis out and show them what I have. The ladies squeal with pleasure. They have never seen such a cock as this. It is five times the size of the average cock. I have had an operation, and four other cocks have been grafted on to my own. The bartender is amazed. He buys me a drink and asks if he may touch it. I tell him only women are allowed to touch this specially constructed member. He is disappointed. I can tell that these lesbians are dying to touch it. A young and pretty thing comes over to me and puts her hand on the head of the huge cock. It begins to get larger, thicker, and longer. The girl hitches up her skirts and tries to get it inside her. The other girls laugh at her, for she cannot get the job done. Other girls try and they fail. The human cunt is not built that can accommodate the hairy dragon that lives beneath my belly. I tell the girls to get out of the way. I stroke myself. The great blue veins running down the long, thick shaft engorge and swell. I come. A great stream of semen shoots out at high speed. Another little modification of mine. I don't come in spurts. I come in one great burst containing five gallons of come. The sperm streaks across the crowded barroom. It crashes into the wall opposite me, knocking a great hole in it. The bartender and all the ladies break into cheers; they have never seen such a thing as I have just done. I drink for the rest of the night on the house. All the women tell me that they have been converted by my giant cock and its power. All the women want me to marry them. The bartender pleads with me to become his lover. We reach a compromise. If they promise to keep me in food and drink for the rest of my life, I will become everybody's lover. Everybody agrees to this proposal. The ladies ask if I can operate on them so they may take this howitzer of mine inside themselves. I produce my knives, and by morning my new loves are ready, including the bartender's ass. I have been living in this bar for twenty years. I drink the finest whiskeys and dine on food fit for gods. When I am not eating or drinking, I am fucking. While I am eating and drinking, they are sucking. They marvel at my youthful vigor. I have neglected to tell them that I am from another planet and that my life expectancy is 100 million earth years. I left my planet because of embarrassment over the smallness of my penis. My fellow creatures on this faraway world from which I come have penises ten times bigger than mine. If these people in the bar find this out, they will abandon me and steal rockets and fly away to Penis Planet, and I will be abandoned with neither food nor drink nor sucking nor fucking to console me.

The women on my planet have cunts the size to accommodate cocks the size and length of telephone poles whose gallonage at orgasm is equivalent to one average-sized earth bathtubfull. For the first ten thousand years of life, the children of my world live inside their mother's cunts. They go to school there, learn to drive there, and are never introduced to their whole fathers. What they see of him is his cock when it comes slamming in every couple of days. The children learn to swim and sail in his semen. Feeding the children for the first ten thousand years is not a problem. They never get hungry during this time. But they do get dirty, as children do everywhere. This problem has been solved biologically. Our women urinate pure well water mixed with the finest Castile soap. When they urinate every thousand of your years, or so, the little ones are scrubbed squeaky clean. Women on this planet are required by law to urinate at only certain times of the day and in public places. In addition to supplying the population of the planet, the women are also the public baths. If you are walking around on my planet and you feel the need to bathe, you approach the nearest woman and ask her to urinate on you. They are always willing to oblige; they never go out in public for any other purpose. Ours is a wet world comprised of four-fifths urine and Castile soap. It is also a very clean world. I would like to go back. The urine there is better. Not quite as tasty as it is here, but very much cleaner and more sanitary. * * * *

4

SADOMASOCHISTIC FANTASIES

WOMEN ARE NATURALLY DOMINANT

This particular fantasy came to me by telephone, and it remains so vivid in my mind that I could report it in all its detail without listening to the tapes.

* * * * I hope this book of yours is seriously intended because I take this fantasy very seriously. My wife and her girl friend are in Europe, and the fantasy is all I have left until they get back.

My wife runs a beauty parlor of a most unique variety. She closes the shop to regular customers at 6:00. From 6:00 till 8:00 she serves only very special customers.

I arrive at the beauty parlor at 6:00. My wife, her girl friend, and several customers are there. My wife requires me to take off all my clothes. She takes off her panties and makes me put them on. She requires me to put on a maid's hat. Then, while she is fixing a customer's hair, she tells the woman that I am her (the customer's) absolute slave. Some of the women require me to lick their cunts while my wife does their hair. One woman always kneels in the chair, and I am required to clean her ass thoroughly with my tongue. Whenever any of the women go to the toilet, I am required to accompany them and remove their panties and arrange them on the toilet. When they are through, I am required to clean them thoroughly with my tongue. Quite often in the bathroom, a woman will tell me to masturbate. I do this and sometimes they will drink my come.

On weekends at home, my wife and her girl friend have card parties. I am required to dress as a maid and do menial tasks around the living room while they play. The women take turns running their hands inside the panties. They squeeze my balls painfully. They sometimes scratch my cock so that it bleeds. I am required to get under the card table and lick all their cunts until they come. When they go to the bathroom at home, I am required to perform the same services for them that are demanded at the beauty shop. But the bathroom is larger at home, so most of the time, the other women stand around and watch me work.

At the end of the card party, someone always finds fault with my behavior that afternoon. I didn't get somebody's asshole clean enough, or I forgot to empty an ashtray, or my hat is on crooked. For these offenses I am taken down to the cellar. They handcuff me and hang me from the ceiling. My wife hits me five times with a riding crop. Her girl friend does the same thing. Sometimes they spit on me. Just before they leave me, one of them puts a spring clip on the head of my penis. Sometimes they let me hang in the cellar overnight.

My wife and her girl friend enjoy a lesbian relationship. They make me come into the bedroom and watch them lick and suck each other and stick dildos into their own and each other's cunts and assholes. They make me clean the dildos with my mouth. Sometimes they order me to masturbate. While I'm coming, they point at my penis and laugh.

Before I leave for work in the morning, I am given two minutes to move my bowels. When I am through, my wife puts a plug up my ass, and I am not allowed to shit again until the next morning. Then I am required to put on a chastity belt so that I cannot masturbate or touch my cock. The chastity belt forces me to sit down to piss.

On weekends when my wife and girl friend decide to entertain other people, sometimes men and sometimes women, they rent me out to other couples. One of the couples is a man and wife. They dress me in panties and maid's hat. I am required to do the housework, the laundry, and so on. The wife watches while I clean the husband after he goes to the toilet. Sometimes he makes me suck him off while she watches, sometimes I suck her cunt while he watches. Sometimes while I'm sucking her, he fucks me up the ass. He makes me clean him off with my mouth when he is through.

The other couple they rent me out to are two black men. I do all the chores for them that I do for the married couple, but sometimes, in addition to fucking me up the ass, they suck me off. But most of the time they order me to masturbate while they watch.

I would describe my wife and me as happily married. We have been married for eight years. We lived together for a couple of years before we got married. I submit to all these things because my wife orders it. I believe that women are naturally dominant and that men should do what women tell them to do.

When my wife and her girl friend get back from Europe, the girl friend is moving into our house full time. I think they are going to require me to live in the cellar. They have not made up their minds yet. You know, while I'm talking to you, I'm getting horny as hell. Are you married? Does your wife require a maid? * * * *

I asked this man if he was reporting fact or fancy. He said that in real life he actually does all these things. Does he *actually* do these things? He obviously enjoys what his wife "requires" him to do (if she does), his partners enjoy his behavior (if it is actual behavior), and nobody gets hurt except him, and he likes (he says) being hurt.

Yet there is, I believe, some evidence that this is pure fantasy. Would the wife and girl friend close up their beauty shop for a month or more? Do beauticians make enough money to jaunt around Europe for an extended period? If they leave him hanging in the cellar overnight, wouldn't he get gangrene of the hands? Wouldn't his scratched and bleeding penis be so painful that he would be unable to masturbate?

IS THIS NORMAL?

* * * * I'm married, I'm straight, and I have this fantasy while we're making love. I've had it for years. I see myself in convict's clothing. My hands are handcuffed behind my back and my legs are chained together. That's it, that's the whole fantasy. It has no sexual content whatever. And yet picturing myself in this situation never fails to arouse me. Should I see a psychiatrist? I'm so ashamed of myself. But just telling you this over the phone has aroused me. I'm terribly embarrassed. * * * *

I told this man that I have discussed fantasies with psychiatrists, psychologists, and other qualified experts. There is universal agreement that there is no such thing as an abnormal fantasy. He queried me closely and at length on the point. I read to him from my notebooks and medical dictionaries and played him part of a taped interview with a psychiatrist. At last he's convinced that his fantasy is not sick and neither is he. He tells me his name. He's a magazine writer I've met. I tell him who I am. He invites me to the Lion's Head, the bar in New York where every writer in the country must make an appearance at least once a year to prove that he's alive. Drinks are on him, he says. He has made me an offer I cannot refuse.

SNAKES AND THINGS THAT CRAWL

I tend not to believe that the following is a recollective fantasy because of the contents of the first paragraph. Herpetology is a small field. From the internal clues of the fantasy, the man would be easily identified by whatever zoo or university he works for and would be fired. Also zoo and university staff members rarely make enough money to allow them to pay $150 for sex.

* * * * I'm a herpetologist. Been fascinated by snakes and other reptiles since I was a child. I have a Ph.D. in herpetology and am reasonably well known in the field. The walls of my living room at home are lined with terraria and tanks. It is one of the largest private collections, I believe, in the country. All the specimens are alive.

What I'm about to tell you, technically, is fantasy because I think about it all the time. It is also reality because I actually do what I'm about to tell you.

I go to lower-class bars to drink several times a month. I'm not a bad looking man and seldom have difficulty in finding a girl at the bar to talk to. In the course of the conversation, I ask if she would be interested in making a little legal money, say $150, for less than a half hour's work. The prospect of making more than a week's pay in a half hour is usually appealing. Sometimes girls will say no and express indignation and walk away or leave the bar in a huff. But about half of them return to ask what I have in mind. I say I can't tell them, but I guarantee they will not get hurt, they do not have to touch me, and I will not touch them. But, I tell them, for the $150 they will have to take their clothes off and I will take mine off.

They always wonder if I have photography in mind.

If they're wavering at this point, I show them three crisp, new $50 bills and tell them we'll both be back here drinking in less than an hour, they'll be $150 richer, and I'll buy the drinks. Almost always, this clinches it.

We get in a cab and go to my place. On the way, I give the girl the money.

When we get there, I spend a few minutes fixing drinks and showing off my collection. I spend another few minutes with Cora, the black snake. I take her out of her case and stick my finger in her mouth to show how harmless she is. I ask the girl to hold Cora in her arms and tell her there is nothing to fear. There's usually some hesitation on the girl's part, but the $150 overcomes it. She holds Cora and, in a few minutes, is quite at ease with her. I tell her to put her back in her case and to take her clothes off except for her shoes. I take all my clothes off and lie on the thick living room rug. I tell the girl to go to the closet I point out to her and to bring in the bull whip she will see hanging there.

She is naked with the whip in her hand. I tell her to go around the entire room rubbing herself sexily against all the tanks and, while she's doing that, she is to call me all the dirty names she knows. When she starts to do this, I begin getting aroused. When she has made love to all the tanks, I tell her to come over to me, still cursing, and beat me as hard as she can.

They always start out with love taps, which don't do anything for me at all. I yell: "Harder, darling, harder, harder, harder. Hurt me, hurt me. I love it. I need it." In a few minutes, the girl gets the idea and really whips the shit out of me. The harder she hits, the better it is for me. When the pain is exquisite and total, I come all over myself.

I clean myself off, and we go back to the bar. Many times a girl gets so excited over what she is doing, she has an orgasm herself. Or she will want to go down on me or have me take her to bed. I like sex only in the way I have just described. I can't get it up in a girl's mouth. I can't get it up enough to achieve penetration. The only way I can achieve an orgasm is by being beaten or thinking about it while I masturbate.

* * * *

BONDAGE

If cruelty amuses you, I'm sure you will find the following the best fantasy in the book. I find it the most repellent. In the manuscript, as originally submitted to the publisher, this was the last fantasy in the book. After having written it, I decided I didn't want to write about men's sexual fantasies anymore. Possibly you will understand why when you have finished reading it.

* * * * I tie her wrists together with a necktie and hang her on the coat rack embedded in the door. I blindfold her and shove things up her cunt and asshole. Big things, like door knobs and Danish candles that really hurt. I put a wide length of adhesive tape around her breasts as tightly as I can. The tape goes all the way around her a couple of times. I have put heavy silk thread around each nipple, pulling it tight and tying it surgically. Her nipples swell, and the pain is intense. I kick her,

banging her into the door. I get the hot water going in the bathtub until it's practically boiling hot. It's too hot for me to touch. I put a towel in. I pick it up with surgical clamps. I just beat the fucking shit out of her with the boiling towel. Every couple of minutes I toss the towel back into the tub and take out another hot one. I can practically come telling you this. She whimpers and moans when the towel thuds into her with all the force I can manage. She screams, and I fear the neighbors will hear. I go into the bathroom and piss on a washrag and stuff it in her mouth. What piss I have remaining, I spray on her.

I tell her she shouldn't have screamed like that. I kick her a couple of times as punishment and whisper endearments to her between each one. I literally kick her till she shits out whatever I've stuffed up inside her. More punishment for her is due for being such a cunt-slob. I jam it back in her roughly and tape the cheeks of her ass shut. I pinch each cheek of her ass, getting myself a little mound of flesh between my fingers. I put diaper pins through each mound and fasten them securely. And I mustn't forget the ankles. Between the Achilles tendon and the ankle bone is a soft fleshy area. I push long needles into this region so that they go all the way through.

Is this turning you on?

I begin unwinding the tape around her breasts. When I get to the nipples, I rip the tape off as roughly and as speedily as I can. When I do this properly, a little stream of urine runs down her leg. Technically, in case you care, this level of pain is called "exquisite." It's pain at its highest, the limit the organism can feel before falling unconscious.

I take the diaper pins out of her, and the needles through the ankles. I untape her ass and take the blindfold off and remove the gag from her mouth. She whimpers softly, and tears stream down her cheeks. With spreaders and forceps, I gently take out of her whatever I have shoved inside. I take her down off the hook and lay her gently on the floor and untie her wrists.

She can hardly speak above a whisper. I put my ear next to her mouth so I can hear. "Please," she says, "please, you promised." I smear her with her own shit, being careful to get some in her mouth. If I am able, I will add my shit to hers.

I jerk off and come on her, standing over her so she can watch.

She calls me at the office the next day. She sounds weak still. "Thank you," she says. "It was a wonderful session. I promise you I won't do anything naughty all week. You'll never have to do it again."

"Whoremouth, cocksucking motherlicker, cuntlapping fart-faced cunt, when did you ever get through a week without fucking something up?"

"Don't you dare call me things like that, you goddamn quack."

And I tell her that that little speech is going to cost her. "You think it was rough yesterday? That's nothing compared to what's coming up this Friday. Maybe a nice douche with boiling water? Would you like that, darling? Do you think it might get that filthy cunt of yours clean at last? Do you?"

"I think it's worth a try, dearest one." * * * *

POTPOURRI

This man called and talked for hours. He has just about every kind of fantasy there is. He assured me that he is heterosexual and straight as an arrow. I tend not to believe him. He gave his age as twenty-seven, and he describes himself as a professional graduate student.

* * * * I was screwing a chick last night. A very tender human fuck. Slow and gentle. She loved it. But in my head, it was pure animal. In my head, she was chained. I wandered the streets looking for someone to fuck. There she was. A stranger. I put my hands around her throat. I told her it was die or fuck. She said she'd rather die. I dragged her into the house, still holding her by the throat, and punched her unconscious. Ripped her clothes off and chained her to the bed. She regained consciousness while I was eating her out. She started screaming. "No! No! No!" she screamed. I put a finger up her ass while I was tonguing her. The no's changed to yesses. I took the chains off. I did it all to her. Everything. When we were through, she told me it was the best fuck she ever had. I didn't even know her name.

I don't understand how I can be so gentle in real life and so brutal in my thoughts. You know how big my cock is? It's just average, I guess. But when I think brutal, I imagine my cock is inordinately big, unrealistically big, like as long as from my elbow to the end of my fist.

I have terrible hostilities. I box as a hobby. I'm a lead puncher, always the aggressor, always jabbing, looking for an opening. When I catch you, you're dead. This is real life I'm telling you about. I've really humiliated some super dudes in the ring. But in my fantasies, I'm the one who gets humiliated. Sometimes when I'm balling I imagine that there's another guy with us. He's doing terrible things to me while I'm screwing the chick. He fucks me up the ass, makes me blow him, pisses and shits in my face, makes me smell his farts. Sometimes he castrates me and stuffs my own balls in my mouth. Can you imagine thinking stuff like this? My behavior is normal, but my mind is something else.

I've got a lot of friends who are gay. Sometimes I let them blow me and rim me. But in my head I'm blowing and rimming them. I've never blown a guy in my life, but I think about it all the time. Someday I'm going to do it. So many people like to blow so many other people, there must be something to it. I don't know when it's going to happen, but sometime soon. I don't have anybody picked out, but I know the type. Not a faggot, but a real he-man stud. Preferably married. I must have had a million blow jobs. I know exactly what I like. That's the kind of job I'm going to do on this guy. And when I'm through, he's going to go ape and just kick the shit out of me and call me terrible names. "Dirty, cocksucking, Jew faggot" and stuff like that. Why do I think things like this? I'm not a Jew. I'm not a cocksucker or a faggot. I don't want to be any of those things. But I do, I guess. At least I think about being all of those things.

You know what I think about when I'm jerking off? I think about going down on chicks while they're finger-fucking me. But when this is actually happening in real life, I imagine myself standing over the girl and pissing on her. I'd love to piss on a girl. It's called "water sports," and I just don't have the nerve to ask anybody. I mean pissing on people is common as hell. It's not even considered freaky. So why don't I have the nerve to ask? Like that girl I was screwing last night. Nice, normal, pretty, sexy lady. How would she have reacted if I said: "You know, ever since I was a kid I've always wanted to piss on a girl and then fuck her. I really like you. Will you let me?" What would she have done? Put on her clothes and gone home? Thrown up? Laughed?

I think about being laughed at because I'm clumsy in bed or my cock is tiny or I've just shit in my pants. I see myself fucking a girl, and there's a whole roomful of people looking at us and laughing. Even the girl is laughing. I'm trying so hard to give her a good fuck, and I can't seem to get it right. I fall out of her or it goes in her ass by mistake or I accidentally piss in her. Thoughts like this can't be normal. I ought to see a shrink.

I see myself with a mustache. Cunt mouth, that's me. I'm sitting in a restaurant. Guys come in singly and in groups. They see the mustache, and they tell me my mouth looks like a cunt. They politely ask if they can jerk off and come on my mustache. They're so polite about it, I tell them yes. There are twenty guys standing in line waiting to come in my face. My whole face and shirt front are soaking with come. The black guys seem to have the most. When one of those dudes comes in your face, you have to hold your breath. Otherwise you'd drown. I think maybe the first guy I suck off is going to be black. I've never seen a black cock. I wonder if they're as big as people say. After I suck him off, I'm going to rim him, and I hope his asshole is dirty. Then I want that big black cock up my ass. I want it so far up there that it comes out of my mouth. And it's got to hurt. No good unless it hurts. Why the fuck am I telling you this? I know I think things like this. But I don't like thinking about thinking about them. I've never told anybody my fantasies before, not even myself. Do you get a lot of calls like this?

If I started masturbating now, would you hang up or would you masturbate along with me? When I was a kid a lot of us guys would get together and masturbate. We called it a circle jerk. Did you do this when you were a kid? I had a math teacher I liked. I always wanted him to jerk off with us. But I never had the nerve to ask him. I'm twenty-seven. He must be thirty-five by now. Maybe I'll call him up, and we can jerk off together. You sound like a really groovy guy. Would you like to be the first man I suck off? You're not black by any chance?

Sadomasochistic Fantasies 131

Look, I know what I'm telling you is turning you on. It's got to, right? I've got a lot of education, I've probably read more books than you have. We have a lot in common. I mean, we're both literate and civilized. If you fuck me up the ass, what's the big deal? And who's going to know? I won't tell my wife and you won't tell yours. It might work out that you actually like fucking guys up the ass. If you only fuck me, you won't get a reputation or anything. I really can't stop myself. My cock is in my hand and I'm moving the foreskin back and forth. Are you playing with yourself? Is there a woman listening to us? Is there a woman there you can put on the phone? I jerk off a lot in front of my women. They like to watch. I've never jerked off over the phone with a woman listening in. If I call back in an hour, can you have a woman there to listen to me? I'm just assuming you're straight. A lot of writers are fags. You don't sound like one. Of course you may not be a writer. You may just like to jerk off while guys talk dirty to you over the phone.

How would you like to continue this over drinks? I'll meet you someplace, and I'll really give you some great fantasies. I'm really in great physical shape. One look at this great body of mine will turn you on. You'll want to fuck me so much you won't be able to help yourself. While you fuck me, I'll tell you some more fantasies. Do you work with a tape recorder? You can turn it on and listen to yourself fucking and me talking. What a way to do research!

Hey, here's one for you. I'm with this guy, see, and we're stoned. We're talking about fucking animals. We're naked and we've been jerking off. I pick up his female cat and eat her cunt. It really turns him on. He jerks us both off. The cat liked it, by the way. That's a fantasy, but it's also a good idea. Do you have a female cat?

Would you like to spank me? I think I'd like that. I see you as a giant, nine feet tall. I am your slave, and I've just fucked up something you told me to do. So you turn me over your knee and spank me with the flat of your hand. We're both naked, and when you turn me over your knee, my cock hangs down and touches yours. We both get hard ons, and when you're through spanking me, you make me blow you, and then you fuck me. It feels so good I may just come. * * * *

BOY/GIRL

* * * * I have this fantasy of sitting in a bar with a magnificently gorgeous girl with tits like cantaloupes. Just as I am about to feel her up and suggest that we spend the rest of the night fucking around, I feel someone's hand in my crotch. I turn around, and there is this young virile guy dressed in black leather. He's not wearing a shirt, just a leather jacket. He's got shiny black boots, and underneath his leather trousers, I can see a mammoth erection. He nuzzles up close and whispers in my ear. We leave together.

He's got a big powerful motorcycle. We both get on and drive out into the country. We drive for miles and miles, and while we drive, I feel his ass and his cock and kiss him on the neck. The feel of his sweaty body and smooth leather gets me so excited I think I am going to come.

We arrive at a big field. He tells me to get off the cycle. He ties me to a tree and strips me naked. He sucks my cock until I come. He forces me to suck him off. I'd do it willingly, but I know what game he's playing, and I go along with it to make it better for him. He unties me and we roll around on the ground fucking each other. After hours of great fun, we get on the bike and drive back to the city, nude. I play with his ass and cock all the way and old ladies stare at us.

I vary the fantasy sometimes. Instead of the cycle, we go to the country on a horse. After we have finished with each other, we take on the horse. We suck it off and fuck it up the ass. The horse's cock is fourteen inches long. His is at least eight inches long.

Another variation is that I am the guy in black leather. No underwear, just hot leather against my skin. I am in the bar, and it's hot in there. I take off all my clothes and turn into a beautiful girl. All the guys in the bar who I had thought were gay are suddenly all over me. Seemingly all at once, everybody's clothes come off, and cocks are rushing at me from all sides. They fuck my mouth, my ass, my cunt, and I'm jerking other people off, all at the same time. The bar is an ocean of slippery sperm. After hours of this, we leave the bar, still naked, and go to another place to get stoned.

On our way, we run into a gang of guys all in black leather. They beat us without mercy, and many of the guys are castrated. I am carried off to the woods. They impale me on a stake up the cunt and whip me. I'm dying, but I'm screaming for more. I jerk off to both these fantasies. As I suppose you can guess, I'm bisexual with a leaning toward gay. I'm a college student. * * * *

Actually, I didn't guess anything except that he was a college student.

ANNUAL SEX

This man wrote me, giving me his name, address, and telephone number. He said he had a sex problem and would like to discuss it with me. I wrote him back telling him that I am not a therapist. I gave him the telephone number of a sex clinic. He called me on the phone several weeks later and again said he needed help and asked if I would at least listen to his problem. He said his problem involved sexual fantasies and real life behavior. The statement of his problem would be useful in my book, he said. In return for the fantasy, he was sure I would change my mind about helping him. With some misgivings, I agreed to listen.

* * * * I'm forty-seven years old, have a high school diploma, and I work as a dishwasher. Have you read *Tom Sawyer?* Remember when Tom is in the classroom and Becky has drawn a picture of the teacher and gets caught and Tom takes the blame? Tom is called to the front of the class, and the schoolmaster switches him with a hickory stick. Well, my fantasy is that the schoolmaster gets sexually aroused while he is beating Tom and comes in his pants. Tom, too, gets aroused by the beating, and he comes in his pants. From this time on, Tom and the schoolmaster become lovers. Tom comes to the teacher's study every day after school and gets a sound beating, and both of them come in their pants. This leads to other things.

You've read *David Copperfield?* Well, David's sister marries Mr. Murdstone (Basil Rathbone did a great job playing him in the film). Well, Mr. Murdstone does not like David. David makes some kind of little mistake, and Murdstone takes him upstairs and beats him with a cane. Well, the same thing happens to Mr. Murdstone and David that happened to Tom and the schoolmaster.

In real life, I am a master. I'm not a lover. I'm a master. I like to find young guys nineteen or twenty years old. I bring them to my room and take down their pants. I lay them across my knees and beat them with a belt. Sometimes I hold their organ when I do this. Sometimes I make them come with my hand.

After doing this I have annual sex. You know, I have sex with them in the annuus.

Well, my problem is this. I've put ads in the papers telling people what I like. People write me and I write them back, but nothing ever seems to happen. I'm not as young as I used to be, and I'm having trouble finding as many young guys as I want. I wonder, do you know how I can go about finding guys who like what I like? I don't beat them hard. I give a kind of parental beating. Like a father beating his son. You know, like a stern master. It's not cruel or anything like that. It's just discipline, is all. Nobody really gets hurt. I think about thrashing young men when I masturbate. I used to have a wife, but she left me when she found me a couple of times with young guys. So I think about Tom and David and masturbate a lot. * * * *

Throughout the conversation the man giggled in spots, and there was a lot of grunting going on. He terminated the call three times, so I imagine he was masturbating while he was talking to me.

At the end of the third conversation, he brought up the matter of my helping him. No, he didn't want the phone number of a clinic; he wanted to come to the office and give me a little discipline and introduce me to the joys of annual sex. He hung up mad. "I give you some good stuff for your book, and you won't give me anything back!"

I'M TIED UP AT THE MOMENT

This man said that he is a twenty-five-year-old musician. He's been divorced seven months. He's decided he'd rather not pretend to be heterosexual any longer.

* * * * It's taken me twenty minutes to dial your number. I'm lying on my living room floor, bound hand and foot. The telephone is on the floor beside me. No, I haven't been robbed. I'm tied up because I want to be tied up. My two lovers do this to me because I like to be tied up. They're not here now. They left about an hour ago. I suppose they're in the bar downstairs drinking and dreaming up what they will do to me when they come back. No, I'm not really tied up, but it's fun thinking about it. Let me tell how I want today to be. My lovers arrive with ropes. They tie me up and kick me in the balls a couple of times each. They kick hard. I scream for mercy. They put a rope around my balls and drag me around the apartment by it. Every now and then they give the rope a good yank. The pain is so great that I shit. While one lover is dragging me around, the other one is hitting me with his belt. It's one of those wide jobs with a heavy buckle. He hits me with the buckle. He hits me all over, especially on my cock and balls. I have a hard on and wish I could masturbate. I tell them this and they laugh. They both fuck me up the ass. They're rough and their cocks are big and it hurts a lot while they're fucking me. It hurts so much that I come. This makes them mad because they wanted to drink my come and I just wasted it on the floor. They kick me in the balls some more just to punish me for wasting good come on the floor.

They take turns sucking me off. While one sucks me off, I am sucking my other lover off. His cock tastes good. I blow each of them four times. My cock is beginning to hurt now, and when I come, it stings. The last time I came, I saw blood on my lover's lips. They are sucking the life out of me through my cock. What a way to die. Sucked to death. I tell them they are killing me. They respond by pissing in my mouth. They pour boiling water on my cock. The pain is so good that I come again. But this time I warned them. Each lover took half my come—and blood. Blood is now dripping slowly out of the end of my cock. Death can't be very far off. I don't want to die, because when I'm dead I won't feel any pain and I love pain. They're fucking me up the ass again. I tell them to free my hands so I can jerk off. They reach around in front of me and jerk me off again and again. Each time I come, it comes out pure blood. A blood come is better than a come come. My lovers' cocks are all bloody, so I guess I'm bleeding out the ass, too.

They have decided I've had enough punishment for a while. They take a bath together and then they bathe me. I know what's going to happen next. They're going to go downstairs to the bar and get drunk. They're really brutal when they're drunk. They're really going to kick the shit out of me when they get back. My big lover promised me that if I bled, he would kick me bloody, and I've bled a lot today. There's a hundred-watt light bulb up my ass, and it's turned on. So am I. The heat is beautiful. It's burning my guts and the room is getting smoky. Both my lovers were Nazi concentration camp guards. They know all the tricks. They know how to make you hurt so much you wish you could die. They know how to keep you from dying.

The last time they came in drunk, they burned a yellow cross on my cock. Not a cross, a star of David. Boy, I shot some load when they did that. I've never had anything hurt better.

You know I'm making this all up. In real life I really did the S and M thing. Also in real life I have a big hard on. Would you like to come to my apartment? I'll play the piano for you, and you can piss on me while I'm doing it. I'll let you watch me jerk off. Well, can I come to your place and jerk off into your refrigerator? I'd like your wife and kids to watch while I do it. Do you have a wife and kids? Can we all have an orgy together? Children are great at orgies. They're so energetic and cruel and inventive it makes you want to cry. Have you had other calls like this? Can you give me some names and telephone numbers? Are you a master or a slave? I love masters. Cruel ones who do terrible things to me. Would you like to give me some orders now over the phone? I swear I'll do anything you tell me. Would you like to hear me talk to myself while I jerk off?

Are you really doing a book, or did you put that ad in the paper to get a lot of obscene telephone calls? Are you jerking off while I'm talking to you? I'll bet you are. Who the fuck would write a book about fantasies? I wish somebody would. I'd love to read a book like that. Maybe I'll write a book like that myself. Hell, I could do a whole book on just my own fantasies.

Now I've told you my fantasies, you tell me yours. Go fuck yourself you dirty cunt. * * * *

If what this man reports are pure fantasies, and they must be or he'd be dead, he's as sane as the day is long. His sanity notwithstanding, I don't think I'd like to meet him.

HOMOSEXUAL FANTASIES/HETEROSEXUAL BEHAVIOR

This man has an M.A. in education and teaches high school. He has never had a homosexual relationship and claims that he has no desire to try one.

* * * * Men come and get me and take me somewhere. They perform acts upon me. They work me over with whips until I'm like raw hamburger. They put my genitals in a vice. They turn the screw until my balls explode. They make me suck them off while they are doing these things. I don't know how to suck a man off, but they teach me. They all have a turn in my ass. Sometimes when I masturbate, I put a finger up my ass to simulate this. It's a good feeling. The men make me lick and suck their assholes. When they're through with me, they tie me on a cross. They all stand around staring at me, laughing and waiting for me to die. Sometimes instead of this, we all sit around and play strip poker. It really turns me on when I lose, and I always lose. These fantasies are a little strange, I guess, but I really enjoy them. They don't disturb me at all. * * * *

OLDER MEN

This guy writes a syndicated gossip column. He told me to be sure to use his name if I use his fantasy. As a matter of ethics, I will not use his name, but I will print his dull and ho-hum fantasy in his exact and unimaginative words.

* * * * I see myself with an older man, someone in his fifties. He dresses me up in stockings, garter belt, panties, and bra. I model for him. He turns on to that. He turns me over his knee for a light spanking. Then I get down and blow him. Then he fucks me. This happens in real life, sweetie. * * * *

THE BUTLER DID IT

This fantasy came in by telephone from a man whose voice I instantly recognized as belonging to a television producer whom I have met a number of times and have watched on television talk shows often. In order to get him to talk to me, I had to lie to him. He asked me if I recognized his voice. I believe he would have hung up on me if I had said yes. So I said no.

* * * * I'm fifty, married, and gay. My wife is a cover. I used to be in the closet, but a year or so ago, I came out. I've joined the movement, I contribute money and time to it. I don't know why I keep my wife. Habit, I guess.

My fantasy life has increased greatly since I turned forty. My sex life has correspondingly decreased, and I masturbate much more now than I did previously. Every four or five months I go on a kind of sex spree that lasts for several days. And sometimes I go for months with no sex at all, not even masturbation. The way I'm living disturbs me. I would like to get some stability in my life. What I'd really like is a steady lover and to stop all this running around I do. I'm worried about the sadomasochistic involvements I find myself in.

My fantasies are mostly S and M. I see myself being spanked, disciplined, slapped, and obliged to perform degrading acts like drinking piss, licking dirty assholes, being shit and pissed on, being forced to perform menial services for big black men who abuse me while I clean their apartments or suck their cocks or do whatever it is they want done.

In one fantasy, I am a little boy. I'm in bed masturbating when the butler comes in and catches me. He's a big black man. Very cruel and violent. He tells me he has to tell my parents. I plead with him not to tell them. I tell him I will do anything he wants—anything.

He commands me to take my clothes off and lie face down on the bed. He spits on my asshole and pisses on it to get it easy for him to get in it. His giant black cock goes in, and I scream with pain. It's like a red-hot poker. I bleed, but he does not stop. He grunts and sweats and fucks me hard. He comes and it stings. Thinking about the fantasy is exciting me. The pain he makes me feel is divine. The harder he fucks me, the better I like it. The more pain he can give me, the better. When he's finally through, he makes me clean his cock for him with my mouth. It's bloody and there's shit on it. I clean him. It's disgusting and I love doing it. I've done this in real life as an adult. I have a special thing for black men—or at least I used to. Back in the fifties, black men were forbidden and thrilling. Today they are less thrilling because it's gotten to be okay to be black. So, today, I have sex with all kinds of men, black and white.

When the black butler is through with me, he takes me to the kitchen and makes me go down on his wife while he watches. While I lick her cunt, he gets his cock up my ass again. She takes a long time to come. He tells me I am doing a bad job on her. He fucks me and hits me. The pain is marvelous, and she tastes and smells terrible. I'm really enjoying telling you this.

I have one fantasy that's so real to me, I don't know whether I'm remembering something that actually happened to me or not. I'm in a canoe paddling up a Southern river. Up ahead of me, kind of far away, is a black man pissing into the water. His limp cock is as big as most men's when they are hard. He has eight inches or so hanging down there. He doesn't see me. I look at that fine cock, and I imagine holding it and kissing and licking it. I wonder how much joy and pain I would feel when he stuck it in my ass. I wonder if I could get it all down my throat.

I'm standing in a bar. A very handsome man about my age comes in. He's white. We have a drink together and chat. He asks me what kind of sex I like. I tell him I like to be dominated and degraded. But I also tell him that I don't really like to get hurt. I like pretend pain. He tells me that is exactly the kind of sex he likes to give. He tells me one thing he loves to do is have his partners drink his piss. We put our drinks down and go into the men's room. His cock is gorgeous. He puts it in my mouth and pisses. I drink for a few lovely moments like this, and then I take it out so I can see the piss stream out of him into me. What a lovely sight it is, and how nice and salty it tastes. I tell him that he must have been eating asparagus, it tastes so good.

We go back to the bar and have some more drinks while he tells me what he's going to do to me and what he's going to make me do when he gets me home. I get a terrific hard on listening to what he's going to do.

There are a lot of people like me and a lot of people who like sex with people like me. There's a whole society of us called the Eulenspiegel Society. We meet on Sundays on Fourteenth Street. We also publish a journal called "Prometheus." You can buy it at the Oscar Wilde book shop. The Society is headed by Pat Bond. That name tells you something, doesn't it? I am stroking my cock while I'm talking to you. * * * *

Like many callers with cruelty fantasies, this man was a giggler. I have asked psychiatrist friends why sadists giggle when in the presence of pain. Do they find humor in suffering? The answer is no; the giggles are an expression of intense pleasure, joy, and glee. The sadist would like to laugh outright but realizes this is socially unacceptable. He suppresses the laughter, and it comes out giggles. Remember the film *Kiss of Death?* Richard Widmark pushes an old lady in a wheelchair down a flight of stairs. The camera does an extreme closeup of Widmark's face. In the background the viewer hears the wheelchair clattering down the stairs and the screams of the old woman. Widmark's eyes light with hellish glee. He giggles. In my mind's ear, I can hear that giggle yet. In the course of researching the book, I heard it many times from many men. Widmark, to his great credit as an actor, reproduced the sound perfectly. The scene is so chilling, because of the giggle, that most often it is excised for television.

SLAVE

* * * * When I come in from a date and throw my coat on the floor, it's a signal to my roommate that I did not get laid. He drops his pants, wipes on Vaseline, and I fuck him. He washes me off and sucks me off, if I wish. He does all the housework and cooking and pays for everything, giving me whatever money he has left over out of his

paycheck. He blows my friends when I tell him to, or gives them his ass to use. If I have a girl over, he is required to bathe us both before and after we have sex. He masturbates on command. If I become tired, and the girl wants more, he has to do what she wants.

When other people are around, he is not allowed to wear clothes. This lets everybody know where he stands. He fixes the drinks, keeps the ashtrays clean, and speaks only when spoken to. He offers his services at my cocktail parties. Fairly often, one or more guests will want to beat him. We keep a large assortment of canes and whips for this purpose.

He's a very good fuck because, when he is not actually on the toilet shitting, he wears a thick plug up his ass to keep it nice and loose. He uses oils and creams on his ass to keep it soft and pliant for everybody. I'm thinking about having him have his teeth removed so he can give a softer blow job.

He sleeps in the bathroom at night. I chain him to one of the legs of the sink. He sleeps on the floor. Sometimes, in the winter, I forget and leave the window open. Once I found him unconscious. His table manners are disgusting. He is not allowed to eat when my friends and I are around. If I have a weekend party, he does not get to eat until it's over. He's usually too busy to eat anyhow. He's a Southerner and really hates blacks. A lot of my friends are black. They really take advantage of him sometimes and make him do crazy things like eat their shit and drink their piss and smell their farts. He doesn't like it, but he does it anyhow. He refused to give a black guy his ass a couple of years ago, and I kept him chained for two weeks to teach him a lesson. I'm trying to get him over his bigotry, but I don't seem to be making much headway.

My friends borrow him, when I go out of town, to do their housework and take care of any sexual needs they and their friends have. And their other needs, too, of course.

One of the funniest things we've ever done with him was make him give his ass to a great dane and then blow the dog afterwards. We took home movies of this and sent them to his parents. How about that for a groove? He cried for weeks, couldn't go to work or anything. I suppose we ought to do movies again. Maybe with a black guy to really shake his folks' tree. They're bigots, too.

He's sort of a one-man band at an orgy. He'll blow one guy, take it up the ass from another, and jerk two guys off, all at the same time. When you consider that he's making the drinks and doing the cooking and waiting on the table too, you get an idea how busy he gets.

As a demonstration of his submissiveness, I had him put the head of his cock over one of the burners on the stove and turn the burner on. Some blister. He had to go to the hospital. I had a party going when he arrived home from the hospital. The first thing I made him do was go to the kitchen and put his cock over the burner again. This time, though, I didn't have him turn it on. I missed not having a servant around. Making your own breakfast is a pain.

We have laundry equipment in the basement. I let him use the driers, but he has to wash all my stuff by hand. Clothes last longer this way, I think.

On my birthday, I always throw myself a big party. One year somebody wondered how many guys he could blow in an evening. He blew twenty-six guys that night before he got sick. While he blows people, we usually let him jerk off. This night, we did not. He was really hurting when he gave out. He asked permission to masturbate, and I turned him down. He still had that hard on the next day. * * * *

MY FRIEND, THE RAPIST

This man talked to me in a bar. He saw the tape recorder and asked if I were a reporter. I told him about the book. When he found out that I lived in another part of the country and would, in all likelihood, never be in this bar again, he agreed to tell me his fantasies provided I paid for the booze. His giggles began when he got to the part about his sister.

* * * * What I'm going to tell you are all fantasies, but I have

lived them all out, too. I like all kinds of sex with all kinds of sexes. But the discipline and humiliation thing is what I like best. I go into bars and pick guys up. I tell them that I want them to take me home and spank me and fuck me up the ass and piss on me. I tell them I have an icebox full of beer that I want them to drink. The more they drink, the more they piss. When one guy is pissing on me and another one is giving me an enema, that's the best there is. Once in a great while, I get real lucky and there'll be three guys. One guy gives me the enema, another pisses on me, and the third spanks me. I really do like spankings. I have leg manacles and handcuffs at home. I take my clothes off and get into the bathtub and lie down on my back. The guy kneels on my chest and pisses into my mouth. I drink his piss because that's what I've told him to tell me to do.

All the guys I bring home are real stud types, masculine all the way. When they spank, they don't fool around. My ass smarts all night.

I have this friend who's a rapist. I go to a bar where nobody knows me. I pick up a girl and take her to a hotel room. My friend is waiting there. The girl and I walk into the room, and my friend springs out at us. We pretend not to know one another. He handcuffs me to a radiator or a pipe or something while holding the girl by the hair. He tells her one way or another, he's going to fuck her. She can scream and holler and give him a bad time, or she can just take it like a man. But no matter what she does, she's going to get asshole fucked, cunt fucked, and she's going to blow him. I really like to watch this guy operate. After he's through with her, he slaps me around, and most of the time he fucks me up the ass and makes the girl watch. Sometimes the girls get real cooperative. He makes me lie down in the bathtub and pisses on me, and then the girl does the same thing. He forces me to masturbate for her. This really turns a lot of girls on, and they get carried away and blow me or let me fuck them just like he did.

He's been deviling me about my sister. She's twenty and a real snot. I've wanted to see her pussy ever since she was a child. We can't work the hotel thing with her, but we'll think of something. I want to watch her blow him and see that stiff prick of his up her ass. Nothing like a cock up the ass to make people less snotty. He's going to make her piss on me and make her watch while he pisses on me. He's going to fuck her up the ass while she's giving me an enema. He's going to force her to jerk me off and suck my cock until she's red in the face. All this is safe because she'd never dare tell our folks that she blew her own brother and pissed on him. I hope she likes it in the ass. I hope she likes it so much that she'll give me some of it any time I want it at home.

My friend the rapist wears panty hose under his clothes. I bet his fantasies are beautiful.

I go to strange bars and ask guys if I can drink their piss. A lot of guys really turn on to this. We go to the men's room and I sit on the john while they piss into my mouth. Guys like this usually wind up spending the night with me. I've had enemas while blowing guys, or did I tell you that? When I can't get a guy, I fuck myself up the ass with a sawed-off broom handle I've got. Sometimes I sleep with it in me. On days I'm not working, I shove it up and walk around with it inside me. I look around for a guy to take it out and make me suck it. As a matter of fact, it's inside me now. I've got dildos and vibrators. I wish I could walk around with the vibrator in, but the damned things are so noisy.

Sometimes my friend with the panty hose fucks me up the ass with a vibrator up his ass. Next to another guy up his ass, he likes the vibrator best. * * * *

5

ASSORTED FETISHES

THE HORSELESS JOCKEY

At a huge drunken bash in the San Fernando Valley, attended by a lot of Hollywood people, I met a thirty-year-old homosexual executive producer. He leaned up against the elegant flagstone fireplace, telling me how important he was and dribbling a martini down his shirt front. He knew I had just interviewed one of his studio's stars that day; he was doing his damndest to work his way into the story somehow. Among other whoppers, he told me the star never made a move without consulting him. He broadly hinted they were lovers. He kept referring to the star's wife as "that bitch," and generally regaled me with all kinds of useless and untrue trivia.

"Did you know that I'm working on a book about men's sexual fantasies?" I asked him.

"Oh, how nice!" he squeaked. "Would you like to hear mine?"

* * * * Well, when I was in the navy, I discovered a funny thing about myself. I have this thing about jockey shorts. Not boxer shorts, mind you, but jockey shorts. And the tighter the better. I made this discovery about myself on my very first day in the navy. The doctors were examining a room full of us, and almost everybody was wearing jockey shorts. I noticed that, as I looked at all those young men in their tight jockeys, I was getting terribly turned on. I had a hard time keeping from getting an erection. The only way to keep my cock from standing up was to stop looking at the jockey shorts and concentrate my attention on the boxer shorts.

Throughout my four years in the navy, I seldom lost an opportunity to go on sick call. That way I got to see all kinds of tight jockey shorts. When I masturbated, then and now, I wear jockey shorts, and I hold my cock in a pair of jockey shorts while I'm whacking away. And when I'm making love, I like my lover to wear jockey shorts. Sometimes I'll pick up a guy in a bar or someplace and he'll be wearing boxers. So I carry a pair of jockeys with me always.

[He reached into his hip pocket, at this point, and showed me the shorts.]

When I got out of the navy, I went to college. I supported myself by selling men's underwear in Macy's. Oh God, what a delicious experience that was! I got to see jockey shorts, I got to sell them. Oh, how I hated to part with the beautiful things. Sometimes I'd go home at night and just cry at the thought of giving them away for money.

While I was working at Macy's, I lived in a dormitory on campus because it was cheaper than having your own apartment. One night during exam week, a bunch of the boys were studying around the clock. They were taking speed to keep themselves awake. Because of the speed and lack of sleep, they started doing crazy things. A bunch of them came into my room and made me take my clothes off, right down to my jockey shorts. They dragged me kicking and screaming to the girls' floor above us. They made me run up and down the halls while the girls pointed at me and shrieked and laughed. I was so embarrassed! But it also turned me on. I got a big hard on, and as more girls stood in their doorways and laughed at me, I got so sexy that I came in front of them, which made them laugh all the harder, those bitches. God, was I mortified! They finally let me go back to my room, and I just shook and shook all night.

One of my best experiences at Macy's was a woman who came in to buy shorts for her little boy. She couldn't remember his size. So I called him on the phone from behind the counter. He said he thought he wore an eight. I told him to look at a pair of his shorts to make sure. He discovered they were actually tens. You can't imagine how thrilling it was to talk to a little boy about his shorts right in front of his mother. I asked him if the tens were tight on him or baggy. When he said they were very tight and he liked them that way, I came in my pants. Too funny! His mother asked me if I were having a fainting spell. Can you imagine?

Do you know I have been subscribing to *Esquire* and *Men's Wear Daily* for years? They're the best places to see pictures of jockey shorts. Also on my days off, I go shopping in men's stores and army/navy stores. I don't buy shorts; I listen to men order them. Sometimes, when a real stud-looking guy spends a long time picking out his shorts, I jerk off right there underneath my raincoat.

You know, I've done a lot of research on jockey shorts. They first came into existence in the 1870s. Back then, they weren't held up by elastic. Elastic came in just before World War II. Remember that cute little red ribbon of elastic jockey shorts had back then? Nowadays you can get them with either red elastic lines or blue ones. I think the reds are much sexier, don't you?

Oh God, do I have fantasies about jockey shorts. I dream about Marlon Brando and Paul Newman in jockey shorts. I have lots of sexy fantasies about what Marlon and Paul and I do in our shorts. Can you imagine how beautiful they must be in their extra-tight shorts? Can't you just see the bulge? * * * *

At this point the little man was getting more than a little steamy. He asked me what kind of shorts I wore. I told him that many years ago I read that Hemingway did not wear any shorts at all. In an excess of hero worship, I had not worn shorts since that day. "My God, you're kidding," the little man shrieked. "How gross! How utterly, utterly gross."

JOCKEY SHORTS REVISITED

I wonder if the people who manufacture jockey shorts know how many people literally adore their product. It seems to me that an advertising campaign could be created to attract jockey short fetishists. The company's profits would skyrocket because the fetishistic employees would work for free, or as in the case of this young man, he'd pay them for the privilege of working there.

* * * * This is really embarrassing. I've never told anybody my fantasies before. I'm not sure how to begin. I'm not even sure I can get enough courage to tell you. You see, I've got this thing about... Say, could we just chat for a few minutes? Why don't you tell me something about yourself or tell me how the book is going or something. My name is _____, by the way. This fantasy is so freaky. I'm not, but the fantasies are. The people in the book are going to be completely anonymous, aren't they? I mean, if I thought there was any possibility that someone might find out... Look, I'm going to hang up now and have a drink. I'm really nervous. I'm shaking. My hands are shaking. I'll call you back in ten minutes or so or maybe never. But I'd really like to tell you about it.

[He hung up and called a few days later. He called late at night. He was very drunk.]

Look, I'm a perfectly normal guy, see. I mean, I'm not a fag, and I don't do anything strange in bed. I've got a good job. I've got a girl, and we're talking about getting married. What we do in bed is all normal. We go to bed and love each other and fuck. She likes to suck me off, which I like, and she likes me to eat her, which is sort of off-turning, but I do it for her anyhow because she likes it so much.

All this sounds normal, right? Well, wait till you hear what I think about all the time. I think about—are you ready for this—I think about jockey shorts. I don't mean I think about them once in a while, I mean I think about them all the time. I think about them when I'm balling my chick. I think about them when I jerk off. I think about them when I'm at the movies, walking in the park. I think about them at work, when I first get up in the morning, and they're the last thing I think of when I go to sleep. For God's sake, I even dream about them. I dream about both kinds, Arrows and Jockeys.

I've been like this since I was a little kid and I don't know why.

Jockey shorts symbolize humiliation for me. I mean, they're just so goddamned silly looking. I mean they're really stupid. I hate to wear them, and I hate them so much, I hate to have other people even look at them. My father and older brother wore them when I was a child. I was fascinated by them. They're so obscene looking. I think I associate them with being a little boy, a baby even. They're a kid's garment, a diaper, that adults continue to wear. Men have an entirely wrongheaded attitude about jockey shorts. They don't pay any attention to them. Women have the right attitude. You show a woman a pair of jockey shorts and you know what they do? They laugh.

I love to be humiliated in my fantasies. My ideal fantasy partner is a fourteen-year-old girl. I would take my pants off in front of her. She'd take one look at my jockey shorts and go all giggly. A better fantasy is when I take my pants off a whole room full of fourteen-year-old girls begins laughing at me. My face gets all red. I'm really embarrassed. I love to be embarrassed. Not in real life. Just in my fantasies.

To intensify the great feeling the fantasies with the little girls gives me, I pretend to myself that I am not willingly taking off my pants. They are forcing me to take them off. The pants come down, and I suffer greatly when they start laughing. I mean, really suffer great humiliation and embarrassment. It's like psychological bondage.

In real life a situation like this would be very difficult to achieve. But I'll tell you something. If I ever got involved in a situation like this in real life, I'd shoot instantly. As soon as the pants came down, off I'd go without touching myself. As soon as they started to laugh, bang! Sperm all over the place. Gallons of it. It would be the greatest come I ever had in my life.

Other fantasies that turn me on are boot camp and fraternity scenes. I see hundreds of guys milling around in their jockey shorts. Old swimming hole scenes where guys are swimming in their shorts.

Did you know that the navy is now issuing both kinds of shorts, boxer shorts and jockey shorts? Jesus, we'll never win any wars that way, I'll tell you. When I found out that the navy is issuing jockey shorts, I went to the local commissary to check it out. They're white, for Christ's sake. Just like civilian jockeys. While I was looking at all those jockeys in the showcase, I had visions of the entire navy walking around in them. I got a hard on just thinking about it.

I bought some jockey shorts from an old woman once. I really wanted to talk to her about which kind I should buy, Arrows or Jockeys. But I didn't want to seem like a pervert or something. I asked her a couple of questions, and it turned out that she really knew a lot about jockey shorts. She got into the details of their design and construction. Standing right there at the counter, I shot my wad. I didn't touch myself or anything. I just came in my pants.

I wonder if this thing I have about jockey shorts has anything to do with something my mother used to threaten when I was a child. She used to threaten to take down my pants and spank me. She did this many times in front of other people. She never actually did it, just threatened. My mother was the disciplinarian of the family. My father was a real cream puff.

Jesus, just sitting here talking to you and thinking about that old woman talking about underwear is giving me a hard on. If I keep remembering that conversation, I'll bet I come without touching myself.

Did I tell you I have a friend who's into diapers? After work on Fridays, he goes home and gets into diapers. The first thing he does when he gets them on is to piss in them. When he has to shit, he shits in them. He doesn't take them off all weekend. Freaky, huh?

Boy, did I tell you about crossing the equator? God, it was great. I was having orgasms all day. They made all us polywogs wear our shorts on the outside of our trousers. There were hundreds of us wandering around the ship like that. I'm sure glad my shorts were on the outside. There was this great big round stain on the front of my trousers. If it hadn't been for the shorts, everybody would have seen and thought I'd wet them. As it was, I was embarrassed to take my pants off in front of the other men. I went to the showers and took them off under the water so the trousers were all stained and nobody would notice the stain in the front.

When I got out of the navy, I drifted from job to job. And the reason I did this was so I would get a lot of physical exams. I love doctors and nurses seeing me in my jockey shorts. I like stern doctors who order you around a lot. When the nurses look at my crotch, it really turns me on.

Did you ever see the movie *The Marrying Kind?* Aldo Ray is in the film. He wears boxer shorts. Hey, wow. That was a groove. He's out on the streets of New York in his shorts. Wonderful! An absolutely unforgettable scene. I've never forgotten it and I never will. Did you see *Unconquered* with Paulette Goddard? She's captured by Indians. They tear her clothes off. I was a kid when I saw it. It terrified me. But there she was, standing right there in front of everybody in her underwear. I loved it, looking at her in a petticoat.

Did I tell you about Macy's? Well, I fantasize that I'm selling men's underwear in either Macy's or Gimbels. Only it's a funny kind of job because they're not paying me. I'm paying them for letting me work there. All day long I talk to women about underwear for their little boys and their husbands and boyfriends. They ask me questions about underwear, particularly jockey shorts. I talk to them by the hour about Jockeys and Arrows. One little boy tells his mother he wants boxers, and she insists that he wear jockeys. I just stand there and listen to them bicker, getting a hard on and shooting off in all directions.

The women standing around the counter and talking about men's underwear are derisive. They laugh and scoff, but they are fascinated by what they are looking at and talking about. In my mind's eye, I see the mothers putting the shorts on their little boys. I can see the bulge where his penis is. The shorts are very, very tight. I can see them, but they can't see me. It would spoil it for me if they could see me or knew what I was thinking.

I want to do a book on the history of jockey shorts. It's a bottomless well of a subject. I want people to respond properly to underwear. Did you know the waistbands of Jockeys and Arrows are different? The best ones are the ones made by Jockey, but the red stripe in the Arrow is pretty nice, too. Different waistbands affect me differently. Jockey is the oldest company in the field. They were founded in 1934. I love their ads. I wish Joe Namath would do an ad for them. I'd go off like a skyrocket. I love seeing pictures of celebrities in their shorts. It's so humiliating. The mighty have fallen.

I keep scrapbooks. Whenever I see the word *jockey,* I clip the item. Even if the word means a guy who rides a horse, I still clip it. I look up words like *underwear, jockey, arrow,* and *underpants* in dictionaries when I have the chance. The word *underpants* is so childish. According to the O.E.D., it came into the language in 1937. The word *briefs* came into the language the same year.

Did you know that *Esquire* has just published a $35.00 book on men's fashions? Four solid color pages on underwear. Beautiful. There's a shot of Ingemar Johannsen in shorts. And Jean-Claude Killy doing yoga in his drawers. Wonderful, wonderful.

I had a girl friend once who was my ideal partner. I should have exploited the situation, but I didn't. She was dizzy and loved to talk about her brother's underwear. When she did, my heart would pound like a drum, and sometimes I'd shoot. Her father wanted her brother to wear boxers and said "Jockeys are for kids." Her father shared my views, which was terribly exciting.

You know what I do every now and then? I go to a YMCA and get a room. I strip down to my shorts and go out in the hall and lock myself out. Then I walk up and down the hall until I hear a man and a woman talking. I knock on the door and tell them I'm locked out. Can I come in and use the phone to get somebody to let me in the room. When the girl laughs at me for being in my underwear, it really turns me on. I go back to my room and jerk off after this. Once I did this. When I got back to the room, I pulled my prick out through the shorts and started jerking off. The man and woman who had let me into their room were walking by my door. The door was shut. I could see their reflection in the transom. As the girl walked by, she glanced up. She saw what I was doing and she smiled. If she'd only waited a second more, she could have watched me shoot. I really shot one hell of a wad that time, it thrilled me so much to have gotten caught.

Did you read *Rabbit Run?* There's this scene of Rabbit going to bed with a woman. He takes his pants off and she laughs at his jockey shorts. Great scene. I've read it and reread it. It's great to jerk off to.

There was a story in *TV Guide* a while back about the gag writers on the Cavett Show. The article concluded that the only funny subject left on TV is jockey shorts. Good article, and I love jockey shorts jokes on TV.

I saw a Paul Anka short some time ago. There was a shot of him in his dressing room in his shorts. There were a lot of women in the theater. They laughed at the sight of him in his shorts. I jerked off.

Sometimes around the house I wear beads and jockey shorts. I like to look at myself in the mirror. I look so freaky and incomplete.

* * * *

I asked this man whether he ever thought about getting a sales job with either Arrow or Jockey. He said he'd thought about it for years. He says he's making a lot of money at what he's doing now—not underwear-connected—and wouldn't want to take the paycut he'd get as a salesman. I told him that his dedication to the product would probably boost him to the company's presidency very quickly. "Then I'd be dealing with lawyers and accountants and stuff and probably never see any underwear again." He concluded wistfully: "Boy, if I weren't making all this money, I'd pay those guys to let me sell underwear. I'd pay them extra if they'd give me a contract saying that I would never get promoted into management."

SUZY BROWN

Suzy Brown is a he. He called using a high falsetto voice and said his name was Suzy Brown. "I am taking a survey for *Women's Wear Daily*," he announced. "If your wife is at home, I'd like to ask her some questions, please." He sounded harmless enough, so I turned on the tape recorder and gave her the phone. Here are his "survey" questions along with its "results."

* * * * When you wear short skirts, do your panties show? Do your skirts ever creep up, letting your panties show? When your panties show, does it bother you? Do you wear a garter belt? Do men look? Do your skirts go up when you get out of a car? Do you ever wear skirts

without panties or panty hose? When you wear panty hose, do you wear panties, too? Do you wear them inside or outside the panty hose? Thank you for answering my questions. I just came. * * * *

I think it's nice when surveys turn up good news.

I ENJOY BEING A GIRL

This man, who calls himself Marion, wants to be a girl. Men make him nervous. He asked if there was a woman with me who would be willing to talk to him. My wife conducted this interview.

* * * * Since I was a kid in high school, I've been convinced that nature, in my case, made a horrible mistake. I have a penis and I should have a vagina. I have girls' clothes at home and wear them every chance I get. I can't describe how much better I feel in them than in a man's suit. Women's clothes are tight and restricting. I like the feeling. It makes me feel very secure and confident. When I'm dressed as a woman and men lust after me, I really like that feeling. I've never had sex with a man, and I don't want to. Only rarely have I had sex with women. I masturbate a lot, and I'm going to a gynecologist. She's started me on estrogen, and I plan to have the transsexual operation in a year. I don't know if this is fantasy or not. Do I really want to be a woman, or am I just kidding myself? I wish I knew. What will happen to me if I have the operation and still don't like men? I suppose I'll just have to become a lesbian. Being a male homosexual would bother me. But being a lesbian kind of appeals to me. A lesbian, to me, is the most female kind of female. They're totally untainted by contact with males, if that makes any sense. Of course, when I'm a woman, all this may change. Maybe I'll meet some man and fall in love, and we'll get married and have children. Oh, yes, it's possible to have children. But realistically I think I will be a lesbian.

I like women to dominate me. I don't mean in any sadomasochistic way. I mean in a relationship between a woman and me, she's the boss. I often think about not having the operation and, instead, finding a strong-willed woman to love.

Something that gives me a great deal of satisfaction is taking my panty hose down and sitting down to go to the john. I'm tall and slender with really good looking legs. I wish I had more bust and hips. The estrogen will give me these.

Once I spent an entire weekend as a girl. I went out of town and spent the weekend with two of my cousins, both girls. We went out to dinner and to parties and nobody guessed. We all loved the experience. I think they got more of a kick out of it than I did.

My business requires that I travel frequently between Washington, Philadelphia, and New York. I have friends in Queens, a married couple, who let me stay with them and live as a woman. They both accept me. I feel so relaxed with them. It's just marvelous.

* * * *

I checked with a number of gynecologists about the possibility that Marion can have children. It is not possible, and none of the roughly 3,000 men who have had their penises removed have had a baby. A man who submits to this kind of surgery emerges woman-like, but she is like a woman who has undergone a complete hysterectomy. Many of the people who have had the operation report that they achieve orgasm, but most do not.

I'M IN LADIES' APPAREL

Several years ago when I was on a plane, I virtually stumbled upon the following fantasy. The tape recorder was in my lap, an earplug was in my ear, and I was furiously taking notes in a notebook. After an hour or so, I finished taking notes, cocked my chair back, and prepared to take a nap. The man sitting next to me asked if I was a writer, and I told him yes. He seemed inclined to talk. Among other things, I told him about this book. He said he would like to contribute to it and would dictate a fantasy into the recorder while I slept. I set up the machine for him, told him to put the microphone close to his mouth and whisper so that no one could hear him above the roar of the winds outside. While I slept, he talked.

* * * * I'm fifty years old and happily married. I'm on my way to New York for a buyers' convention. I'm in ladies' apparel. This is a great business for me to be in because I'm literally crazy about women's clothes. I have closets full of them at home.

At the end of a working day, I drive home and my wife and I have a couple of drinks. Then I go upstairs and change clothes for the evening. I put on panties and panty hose and, usually, a long dress and padded brassiere. I put on some perfume and whichever wig I feel like wearing that evening and go downstairs and start fixing supper. While I'm cooking, my wife keeps the drinks coming. After four or five drinks, the two of us get loosened up, and it becomes easier for us to really turn things around. I pretend I'm the wife, and she pretends she's my husband. She tells me about her imaginary day at her imaginary office. I tell her about the shopping I have done during the day, what the ladies said at my imaginary bridge club, who is having affairs with whom, and all the other details of my secret and imaginary life.

Quite often while I'm working at the stove, my wife will come up behind me and play with my "breasts." Sometimes she talks dirty for me and tells me things like "I want you to suck my cock." And "After dinner I'm going to fuck you up the ass." And "Let's do it dog fashion tonight." When she talks like this, I really get aroused, because what she is really saying, what she is really telling me, is how she wants sex that night. Sometimes she plays with my penis while I'm cooking. It gets hard and she knows she's doing a good job of getting me hot. "Tonight I'm going to eat your pussy until you scream for mercy," is one of her most stimulating lines.

Sometimes we get ourselves so hot that we forget all about dinner and rush upstairs and fuck like a couple of rabbits and then come downstairs later.

During sex she takes the man's role. She slowly undresses me and talks dirty to me. She likes to suck me off. Sometimes she does it twice in one evening. She says she likes sucking me off because it makes her feel like a man. She knows that many men are cocksuckers. She also likes it when I fuck her up the ass. She likes to pretend she's a man then, too.

Have you ever heard of anything as weird as this? We're both extremely shy about talking about what we do. Years ago we thought we were crazy. We both went to a psychiatrist. We gave him $50.00 in cash and called ourselves Mr. and Mrs. Smith. We told him what we do when we're at home alone. He told us not to worry about a thing. He told us that love play differs from couple to couple, and that while what we have invented for ourselves is a little unusual, we have nothing to worry about. It makes us happy and doesn't do anybody any harm.

Every now and then the two of us wonder if there are other couples like us. But we're too shy to seek them out. I don't think we'd like to have sex with other people, but it would be a lot of fun, we think, to have other couples like ourselves over to the house, and we could all switch roles for a social evening.

That psychiatrist asked if my wife gets dressed as a man. No, she does not. But she keeps her hair short, and she generally wears slacks. She tried dressing up in my clothes. She says they are uncomfortable and they don't fit. She had a suit tailor made for her. She only wore the suit a couple of times. She said it made her feel silly.

So not only do I *have* fantasies, I live them out.

I hope you find this useful in the book. Good night. * * * *

THEY'RE WRECKING MY MARRIAGE, MY LIFE

Fantasies are supposed to be fun. They're supposed to make whatever kind of sex you do better. Better for you and better for your partner, if any. Sometimes, unhappily, fantasies get out of hand. Sometimes the fantasies are so intense that they interfere with behavior, and instead of making life better, they make things worse. In this man's case, his fantasies were destroying him. He took the telephone number of a sex clinic. For his sake, I hope he used it.

* * * * I'm a fetishist. Any item of women's clothing, that is the sight of women's clothing and the feel of it, arouses me. I've always been like this. When I was a child, I used to borrow my mother's clothing, shoes, stockings, brassieres, anything, and look at them while

I masturbated. I'm married now and I'm doing it with my wife's clothes. She doesn't know what my fantasies are, but she does know we're not having any sex. I've started taking items of her clothing to work. I go to the men's room and masturbate. There's no reason for me to do this. She's a very loving woman and provides, or at least provided, all the sex a man could want. Trouble is, I don't want sex with her anymore. The feelings I get when I masturbate while looking at a shoe, for example, are so much more intense.

I've started stealing women's clothing at work. Handkerchiefs, Tampaxes, and other small things that go unnoticed. I masturbate at work several times an hour. Someday, of course, I'll get caught and fired. But even if I don't, the quality of my work has slipped so much that I'll probably get fired anyhow. Masturbation requires energy. It expends energy. I'm masturbating thirty to forty times a day, and I'm exhausted. My arm is tired, my penis is sore, my brains don't work right. I'm so tired.

I know the world considers fetishists deviant. It's getting harder to conceal what I am. My wife and the people at work think I have bladder trouble that requires me to go to the bathroom frequently. Just before I called you on the telephone, I masturbated while holding one of my wife's stockings. When I get off the phone, I'll do it again. That's sick. What's the technical name for being forced by your psyche to do things against your will? Compulsion. Right. That's it. I simply can't help myself. It's like drugs or alcoholism.

Your advertisement says you're an author. You're not by any chance a therapist, too? I guess you can tell, I'm not calling you, really, to be helpful for your book. I'm calling to be helpful to myself. Can you imagine being forced to have thirty to forty orgasms a day? I'll have a heart attack or get cancer of the prostate if I don't stop and stop soon. Would it help if I told my wife? I think she might be frightened or repelled. I love her and don't want to hurt her. Hurt her any more than I am hurting her now, that is.

This is a nightmare. It's like being pursued by a demon, and the demon is me. It's frightening to be out of control. You have no idea what it's like. I have a picture in my mind now of me masturbating. All hunched over and gasping with pleasure when the orgasm comes. It's ugly. And the pleasure isn't pleasure or even relief. What I'm doing is automatic. It's like I'm a piece of machinery. Remote, alone, impersonal. I'm like an orgasm machine. Orgasm after meaningless orgasm. No love or warmth or pleasure. Something goes click in my head. I see a woman's hat or something and I'm no longer me. I'm that machine that spews out orgasms. I tell you it's horrible, horrible.

Yes. When I get off the phone, I'll call the clinic. Maybe they can see me today. * * * *

SICK

* * * * I am married, happily, and have two children. I am forty-two, a college graduate, and I'm five feet, ten. For the last year I have been having a fantasy that I am a baby in diapers sucking on a baby bottle. I have an erection now as I write this to you. In the fantasy, the baby bottle is full. When I empty the bottle in the fantasy, I come in real life.

I don't like the fantasy, but I can't seem to stop myself having it. It's embarrassing and I'm sure I'm sick. I want to act it out. I'm one of those people who is willing to try anything once. Someday I will act it out. Disgusting, I know. Where does one find a diaper big enough for a five foot, ten man? I find this so stimulating to confess that I probably will ejaculate in a minute or so without touching myself.

My wife is my closest friend. I wish I could tell her about the fantasy. I have it just before we make love. If I told her, she'd be disgusted and probably leave me. Or have me committed.

I'm writing to you from the office so she won't find out. I came in my pants. I'm a damn mess. The mess in my pants is nothing compared to the mess in my mind. Surely I am going crazy. I can't help myself. Sane men have gone crazy before, I know, but I never thought it would happen to me. * * * *

I'm writing this in 1974. This book will not be published until the spring of 1975. By that time, what pain will this man have needlessly inflicted on himself?

A THIRTY-ONE-YEAR-OLD VIRGIN

* * * * I'm, believe it or not, a thirty-one-year-old virgin. I guess I'm gay, but I don't really know. I've never had a sexual encounter with anyone. Except myself. I masturbate every day, frequently more than once. When I masturbate, I think about handsome men I have seen. I think about being in their clothes. I undress myself and them and put on their clothes. The clothes are still warm. The men and I don't do anything. I just wear their tight, warm jeans and get a tremendous hard on when I think about it. I'm thinking about it now and I am erect. I'll masturbate when I finish. * * * *

THE TELEPHONE

* * * * Will you rub the telephone on the front of your pants, please? Will you rub it against your pubic hair? Can we masturbate together while we talk? You can fantasize about me and I can fantasize about you. Please make sounds when you come and hold the phone so I can listen to you breathe. No shit? You're really doing a book? On the level?

I have this thing for phones. I call people, men and women, and ask them if it's okay if I talk dirty to them and masturbate while I do it. A lot of people say yes, and we masturbate together. Sometimes we actually get together and masturbate while talking to someone else on the phone. There are some girls who live on this floor. I wish they'd gang up on me and make me fuck them. One right after another. And then eat them, one right after the other. And then they all blow me. I jerk off to this one almost every night. Through the walls, I can hear the

girls fucking. I hope they can hear me jerking off. I make a lot of noise when I come. I'm sure they can hear me. Do you have a hard on?
* * * *

THREESOME

This one comes from a Democratic district leader from a large midwestern city. He's a real Ivy Leaguer, button down type. He owns his own business and is making a fortune at it. He refers to the people in his district as clods and shit kickers. He has the requisite wife, two children, and large dog. He also has a mistress by whom he has a child.

* * * * I don't know why, but airplanes really turn the ladies on. Most people have never been up in a small plane. They regard it as a real treat when I take them up. First the women are scared. Little planes bump more than big ones. And they're noisier. But once I get to altitude and let them fly it a little bit, they calm down and really get to like flying. But the sex thing is really wild. Once their fear is gone, their sex drive takes over. I can't tell you how many hand jobs and blow jobs I've had from women in that plane. Couple of weeks ago I was flying along and this committeewoman asked if I had automatic pilot equipment. I'd just met her that day. She wanted to know if it was safe to let the plane fly by itself. I told her that if I filed IFR it's perfectly safe. Controllers know where you are. They keep you and other traffic separated. She said, and these are her exact words, "I don't know what's come over me, but will you take me to the back seat and fuck me?" I filed, put her on autopilot, and obliged the lady not once but twice. Happens all the time, and I think about it a lot. The plane turns me on, too. Sometimes, when I'm by myself in the plane, I masturbate. When you're at ten or eleven thousand feet, it's a good jerk off. The oxygen content in the bloodstream is way down and you feel sort of dreamy, like you've just finished a real fine joint of the really good stuff. I pull out my pork and put some mood music on the RDF and do a real slow whackerino. Because everything is slowed down, it takes a long

time to come. When you finally do come, it lasts a long time. The sperm doesn't spurt out as hard as it does on the ground, but there's a lot more of it. I think that's because of the anoxia. It works the same way when you're fucking. And when a girl is blowing you at ten thousand feet, she really has to work for her supper. But if she really likes to eat sperm, it's worth it, all the extra work, because she gets so much extra come. They're less likely to gag, too, because it comes out so nice and slow.

When I jerk off in the plane, I always do it to the same mental picture show, which goes like this: I'm home in bed and a girl calls me on the phone. She's a stranger and she's gotten the wrong number. She tells me I have a sexy voice, and I tell her I'm a very sexy guy. She asks when was the last time I got laid, and I tell her it's been weeks and I'm in a very bad way. I could really use some loving today.

She gives me her address and I go over. She has a roommate, it turns out, and none of us have been laid in a long time. She lifts up the roommate's skirt. She has no pants on. I start taking my clothes off, and the girls begin kissing each other and touching and fondling each other's breasts. When I get my clothes off, I start undressing the girls. They are now eating and rimming each other and it's hard to get the clothes off without disturbing them, but I manage. One of the girls begins sucking me, and the other one says it's okay for her to suck me, but I am to tell her a couple of seconds before I come. That way, she says, one girl gets the fun of sucking me and the other one gets the fun of tasting me. Well, this starts a fight between the two. They both want everything. I sense that things could get nasty and I suggest a compromise. I tell them I'll lie on my back and they can take turns sucking me. Each one gets to start on the head and go as far down as they want and all the way up again. Then it's the other's turn. When I come, each girl gets half. They go for the idea.

By the time I'm coming in the fantasy, I'm coming in real life. I pretend that my hand is moving my cock from one girl's mouth to the other.

I think about threesomes a good deal. Having one girl blow you while another's sitting on your face is my idea of heaven. The wetter the girl is, the better. I really love the taste of a wet lady. In the last century, men believed that when women had an orgasm they came just like men. You know, a lot of fluid shoots out. Well, it doesn't really happen that way. But when they come, some fluid actually is discharged and the cunt sort of relaxes. I've felt this many times and it's a fine feeling. When you get it, you know you've really made the lady happy. * * * *

CHOCOLATE

* * * * She puts two or three Baby Ruth candy bars in her mouth at once and chews them until they're all soft and mushy. She lets the brown and nutty mush ooze out of her mouth. I lick it and smear it all over her body and lick it off. * * * *

The symbolism of this little horror is obvious and needs no elaboration.

THE TEASE

This man describes himself as married, twenty-four, a high school graduate, and heterosexual. His fantasies, which he translates into behavior frequently (several times a week), are unknown to his wife. But he concedes that she "thinks there's something funny going on with me."

* * * * I like to go to public men's rooms and watch men handling their dicks. Some guys hold them with thumb and forefinger, others hold the whole shaft, and some guys don't hold them at all, just let them hang there. When they're through pissing, some guys shake off the last few drops, and others skin it back and milk it forward. Some guys don't bother about the last few drops.

I wink at the men and try to turn them on by taking my dick out and moving the foreskin back and forth until I get a nice erection. The men want to touch my cock and suck it. Sometimes they get down on their knees, begging for it. But I won't let them touch me. I let them get so close that I can feel them breathing on my cock. When they're really going crazy, I jerk off and leave.

Do you think this is crazy?

I like to expose myself to girls on the street. Some girls laugh and some girls turn away. I understand this is considered illegal. I can't see why. Men and women like to see each other, don't they? And they like people of the other sex to look at them, don't they? So all I'm doing when I let them look at me is giving them the chance to do what they all want to do anyway. I have such a lovely cock. Maybe someday you'll get to see it. * * * *

COCK

Who this man is, I don't know. He's one of the men who called in response to advertising. In the long course of researching the book, I never spoke with anyone so single-mindedly devoted to one small part of the male anatomy.

* * * * The love of my life is cock, my own and other people's. I like to look at them. I like them in my mouth and ass. I have never seen a cock I didn't like. Big ones, little ones, children's, black ones . . . I love them all.

I'm lying here naked while I'm talking to you. I'm looking at my own cock, and I'm trying to imagine what yours looks like. Men with nice voices always have beautiful cocks. Will you take yours out, if it's not out already, and tell me about it? Well, let me tell you about mine. From base to tip, it's eight and one-quarter inches long. It is milk white and the head is purplish red. It is an inch and three-quarters in diameter, and it smells like Ponds cold cream. That's what I clean it with, the same cold cream my mother uses on her face.

I'm in the publishing business. I publish gay porn. I have more photographs of cocks in my files, probably, than any other man alive. When photographs of cocks come into the office, they are dated. If they are not used in a year, they are thrown away. Or at least, that's what they think in the office. Actually, about once a week a hundred or so glossies are thrown away. They stuff them in a box and leave them for the cleaning staff to get rid of. Well, the cleaning staff never sees them. I take them all home. I must have ten thousand photographs of cocks here in the apartment. I spend hours poring over them and masturbating. Not only do I have photographs, I have statues, and dildos, and water colors, and oils, and bronzes of cocks in every conceivable state of erection and flaccidity. And movies. I forgot the movies. I have miles and miles of color film of cocks. Soft ones and hard, throbbing and still, large and small, every kind of cock you ever thought of. I have one solid half hour of cocks coming. I have side views, front views, bottom views of cocks coming. I have some sensational shots taken from between men's legs in which you see the divine sperm shoot out several feet. The balls are tight in and blurry, but the head of the cock is in focus, and you can see the jism flying a couple of feet into somebody's mouth. (Nobody's come ever gets wasted here.)

Oh, my own cock, that beauty, is listening to me talk to you, and the dear thing is bobbing up and down trying to get my attention. Behave now, my darling, I will take care of your every wish shortly just as . . . Bill dear, I will take care of yours, if you will only let me.

Would you like to come over and see my come movies? I've never met a man, gay or straight, who could watch the films without letting me suck him while he watches. There is one shot that never fails to get them all, no matter how straight they are. The camera lens is just inches away from the soft cock (it's my cock, by the way), which just hangs there waiting for my hand. The head, all pink and lovely, is just peeping out of the foreskin. It looks so clean. My hand appears. It has mineral oil in the palm. It caresses the sleeping giant and moves away so the camera can get a good view of it beginning to stir a bit. They viewer sees it glisten. I begin stroking myself with thumb and forefinger only so that all of the little man can be seen. Slowly, oh so slowly, I begin the stroke, out and back, out and back. The little pink head grows large and its color deepens. It is now no longer hiding shyly in the protective foreskin. It stands before you boldly.

Are you following what I'm telling you? Do you have a picture of what the film shows? My cock is not yet fully erect. It is pointing straight out at the lens. When fully erect, the camera will see the underside, as it bobs and throbs. The mineral oil is beginning to soak in now. I pour more on and spread it over the ruddy surface of the cock, the head of which is now turning that purplish color I was telling you about, and the shaft, which only a moment ago was an alabastar white, is taking on a ruddy glow of health. The blue veins are filling now, and they run down the shaft supplying fuel for the fires that are now beginning to rage within my glorious instrument.

The lighting in this sequence is fantastically good. You can see every single detail, the stretching and wrinkling of the foreskin as I stroke, the flattening and broadening of the head when my thumb and forefinger apply their gentle, expert pressure. And now, a new kind of action comes into view. A tiny drop of clear fluid appears on the tip. As I stroke forward, the drop grows larger. It hangs there quivering, impelled by gravity to begin to ooze down but obviously not wanting to leave the tip. The little drop moves, and on my next forward stroke, it is spread about the base of the cock by the now urgently moving foreskin. The base of the head of the cock is now shiny and sticky with the white fluid.

My hand wants to fly, but I keep it moving slowly and deliberately. I am not satisfying myself, I am providing the world with art. I pour on more mineral oil, and the monster glows anew. Unconsciously, my hand moves almost imperceptibly faster, and the grip of thumb and forefinger increases. The mind guides the hand to new heights of pleasure. Forward and back, forward and back, the gentle strokes follow upon one another like the tides. The head of the cock, now royal purple in color, bobs and weaves in front of the camera lens and gathers strength for its great efforts that will shortly begin. The colorless fluid is now coming out in a stream. Little droplets appear with each forward stroke.

The climax is coming. The colorless fluid is changing color. It is becoming whitish. Finally it changes to a pure mother-of-pearl. A large solid-looking gob of mother-of-pearl appears. It is pushed out by the one behind it and falls out of view. The gob behind it is larger and comes out more urgently. The next one is in such a hurry to come out that it bursts forth two or three inches beyond the cock's head. And the next three are explosions. The first comes rushing toward the camera and hits the bottom of the lens, making the bottom quarter of the picture frame blurry and the color of skim milk. But you can still see the practiced stroking that brings the second explosion. It rushes true and straight to the center of the lens, and for a fraction of a second, you can see nothing but a whitish blur. Through the blur, you can see the third gob of come rushing at the lens. Splasho! Bullseye! The world is white and blurry.

The blur clears as the come drips down. Sperm is pumping out with each stroke, but it diminishes as you watch, and so does the size of the cock. Coming is exhausting work. Come drips. As the stroking continues, the cock's head gets foamy, as if someone put shaving cream on it.

The cock is now at rest. It hangs its head and rests upon the pillow of the hairy balls and goes to sleep. You can tell by looking at it that, though it rests, it will be ready for more work shortly. A cock that comes like that is in perfect physical shape, lean, lithe, and lickable, conquering paradoxically every time it is beaten, singing with pleasure when it is flogged.

Bill, you know your cock is hard now. It stands up despite you. You may not want it down my throat, but it knows better than you. Are you alone? Is your cock in your hand? Tell me where you live. I'll bring a projector. I'll show the footage on your wall. You hold me by the head and bang me into you. Drive your cock down my throat and give me all your come. But don't come down my throat. When you come, come in my mouth so I can taste it. You know, I bet writers build better come than anybody. They sit and they write. They work quietly, and the come factory goes about its work while the rest of the body sits quietly.

God, I'll bet writers come gallons. Do you think you will use this in the book? Do you want pictures of cocks to illustrate it? Well, you can't do a book like yours without pictures. Nobody would buy an unillustrated sex book. And if you expect to sell to the gay market, you better have a shot of a great big cock right on the cover. I mean a big one, baby, with a drop of come on the end.

Look, I'll tell you what. Give me your address and I'll mail you a photograph of my cock. If that won't get you over here to see the film, you're probably impotent. And let me give you my address. Come on a Kleenex for me so I can at least smell it. Couple of pubic hairs would be nice, if you can manage it. Do you have a wife or a girl friend? Can you get all the way down her throat? * * * *

COCK II

* * * * I think about cocks all the time. I make pictures of them in my mind. They're all big, erect ones, and they're beautiful. I see them coming off in my face.

I see myself with a man. I suck his toes and lick him behind the knees. He turns over and offers me his asshole to lick. It's a beautiful rosette, pink and clean and nice. While I'm licking it and getting my tongue inside it, I hold his cock and gently stroke it. I tell him not to come. I tell him I want him to come in my mouth. No matter how much he comes, I will drink it all, even if I strangle. When I say these words, I feel his big cock squirm in my hand, and I know my words arouse him.

Would it interest you to have a demonstration? Would you come over and let me show you what I'm talking about? Have you ever seen Marlon Brando's cock? I'll bet it's just huge. I think about his cock when I masturbate.

I like men to tell me what to do. I'll do anything a man asks of me except the cruelty things. Anything. Once I picked up a marine sergeant in a bar. He was perfectly straight. I took him home. He took off his clothes and got into the bathtub and told me to piss on him. I didn't want to do it, but I was his host, after all. It was my duty to please him. I asked him if he'd let me suck his cock. It offended him that I asked. He said he thought that men who let other men blow them were queers.

Marlon Brando is a policeman. He arrests me. He leans me up against a car, spread-eagled. He frisks me, makes me drop my pants. He fucks me up the ass. I can't see his cock but I can feel it, and it's just gigantic. At the last minute, he pulls out and comes in my ear. I hate to lose it. Later, he goes down on a woman and I go down on him.

It's exciting reporting this to you. I'm going to masturbate when I finish talking to you unless you'd rather I masturbate while we're talking. I have a friend who likes this. We masturbate over the phone together.

I have an idea. If you wouldn't like me to show you personally how much I like cock, would you like to watch me demonstrate on someone else? I can call up a couple of friends, and you can come over and watch us play. Well, if you ever decide you want to be done for trade, let me know. My telephone number is ―――――. Done for trade means getting your cock sucked. For a man doing the kind of book you're doing, you don't know very much, do you? Good night, darling. I'll be thinking about your cock. Have you ever had a blow job while you're typing? * * * *

I AM A DOG

My wife and I have a friend, a writer, who was kind enough to read the manuscript to check it for errors. She tells us that she can't get the following fantasy out of her mind and she's trying to screw up enough courage to ask her boyfriend to do this to her. At the time the book went to press she hadn't asked him yet.

* * * * I enter a room. Someone from behind me, a person I cannot see, suddenly places a heavy, tight blindfold over my eyes. I cannot see. Not even a glimpse of light shines through, and I am in total

blackness. Then, the person begins to unbutton my shirt and remove it, all very gently and slowly. The unknown undresser next unzips my pants, and I sit down so that they too can be removed. My shoes and socks are taken off one at a time, slowly and gently. I am terribly delighted by this. Only my jockey shorts remain. These are not removed. I feel happy and blissful. I am now ready for the transformation, naked except for my underwear. I feel utterly peaceful. I am in paradise. The whole fantasy thrills me enormously, even as I'm writing it to you.

My unknown undresser now places on my feet what feel like white wool socks and heavy boot-like laced shoes like those construction workers wear. This sends twinges of joy through my whole body. I am wild for white socks and laced boots. This is really heaven. Wow! It's really a fabulous feeling.

My undresser now tells me to make a fist of both hands. The voice is male, the first notion I have that the person bringing me to such ecstasy is male. I am still tightly blindfolded and cannot see a thing. My undresser now informs me that I am about to become a dog.

I am intrigued, fascinated, delighted.

My hands are now in fists and my soon-to-be master winds heavy, strong adhesive tape around them. He uses lots of tape to assure that I cannot move my fingers. These are to become paws. I love it. My master tells me that I am not to speak. I am not to act as a human but as a dog. God, what a thrill this is! He applies more tape to my hands and wrists so that the wrists become rigid and immovable. He puts a tight stretch sock over each hand. They are now truly paws. It is a glorious feeling to have paws. My master puts a heavy leather collar around my neck. A short leash is attached to it. He commands me to get down on all fours, to crawl like a dog. What joy! I *am* a dog, and he is my master. I am still blindfolded, and the combination of paws, collar, sweat socks, and boots really thrills me. To write about it is sensationally good, sexually stimulating.

My master now removes the blindfold, and I discover, to my pleasure and surprise, that he is very much like me—young, handsome, and slim. He is also dressed rather like me. Tennis shorts, laced boots, and white socks. Wow! Terrific! This is *it!* He is gentle. He walks me around the room with the leash. He throws a ball and asks me to retrieve it with my mouth. I do this for him happily. I am a good dog and love to play with my kind master. He ties me to a piece of furniture so that I have to stay on all fours and brings me a bowl of crackers to eat and a bowl of water to drink. I eat and drink and do everything he says. When he says bark, I bark. When he says get up on your hind legs, I do it. Glorious, glorious. I am truly a dog.

He is a good master. We have no sexual contact. He treats me like any ordinary dog-owner. He pats my head and my back once in a while and that's it.

I am aroused just by writing this. In real life, I want to be a dog. I wonder how long I could stand it. With a master like the man I picture, I think I could act it out a very long time. I just can't communicate to you how much I want this. I do. I do. I really and truly want to be a dog with a handsome master who wears tennis shorts, laced boots, and white socks. I want to run and play on all fours and eat and drink from bowls.

I'm a practicing attorney, thirty-six years old, and have been happily married for eleven years. My wife and I love each other. I love her in the sack, but, after eleven years, sex gets to be a bit of a routine thing. I've never had a homosexual experience. In addition to my wife, I have slept with two other women, both when I was in college. The thought of touching a man erotically is nauseating, but, with this crazy fantasy of mine, maybe I *am* gay and don't know it.

I want you to know I'm dead serious about this fantasy. I really want to have this experience I have just described to you. I have been trying to find a way to live it out for years. I truly hope that one day I will succeed. * * * *

Counselor, don't worry about being gay. Homosexuals are people who do have homosexual sex, not people who merely think about it. If fantasies were related to behavior in any way and people could be arrested for what they think but don't do, I would be writing this book from prison. I used to think about murdering my first wife all the time. I ran her down with cars, hurled her off bridges, poisoned her soup, bashed her with hammers, strangled her, hanged her, and, a couple of times, I kicked her to death. I am not in prison, and she is alive and well.

THE EXORCIST

* * * * I come from a country where women prize their virginity and save it for their husbands. Many of the men there are virgins when they get married. It is not as burdensome as you might think. My countrymen get married very early. Twelve and thirteen years old is not thought to be too young. When they get married, they are given illustrated books that show them the positions. Their parents provide the books and also the requisite items for stimulation. Because they get married so young, their active sex lives are much longer than Americans. But more importantly, their sexual lives are legitimized. They do not have the guilts about sex that American women have.

In my country, American women would be regarded as whores, because American women have sex with many, many men before they get married. For this reason, American women are unclean. They feel unclean because they have been stained by so many men.

Many American women stop having sex because of their uncleanness.

My countrymen are mystics. We believe in the efficacy of ritual and prayer. When I meet a woman who is unclean and will not have sex with me, I tell her it is possible for her to be reborn, to become pure again, to become a spiritual virgin.

I have a prayer rug and a holy shawl. I tell the woman to remove her clothes and lie upon her back. With many soft pillows, I prop her nether parts high into the air. I kneel besides her and commence reading prayers in Urdu. I insert a candle into her vagina and light it. I read more prayers to her, prayers of purification, prayers that ask for forgiveness for the unclean life she has led. I explain the prayers in English, too. I tell the girl to concentrate on the flame of the candle. I tell her to think about purification by fire, how fire cleans all it comes in contact with. I tell her her vagina is being cleaned, that her soul is being cleaned.

When the candle has burned low enough so she can feel its heat between her thighs, then she is truly clean again. I remove the candle, and she is a virgin. She has become innocent as a child. I tell her that I am the priest who has made her clean. It is not soiling to tend to the bodily needs of the holy man who has cleaned you, I say. The girl lies with me and becomes cleaner than before. * * * *

CRUELTY

* * * * I'm really into cruelty. My sex life is normal, but the things I think about are not. Have you read *Torture Garden?* There's a great scene in it. A man is tied to a stake in an arena and a toothless old crone sucks him to death. Toward the end, he is having a continuous orgasm that increases and increases in intensity to the point that his entire body explodes through his penis, his blood and guts just come shooting out of him. The height of pleasure and pain is to have an orgasm so intense it kills you.

My body is covered with gashes, welts, and scars. I've had to go to the hospital several times to have my asshole stitched up. Sometimes the damage has been inflicted by other people and sometimes by me. I love being fist-fucked. It hurts like hell at first, which is the best part. When the entire arm gets in, the pain is blinding. Great! When the guy gets in and the shoulder starts punching its way in is the best. Once, just as I was coming like this, one of the guys kicked me in the balls. The pleasure was so great, I started screaming.

Once they tied and blindfolded me and turned some kind of animal loose on me. A goat, I think, from the smell. The animal fucked itself to death in my ass. I bled for days and the blood turned the guys on and they fucked me, one by one, for hours.

I dig children. Boys and girls. I give them liquor, and when they're too drunk to fight me off, I bugger the shit out of them. Literally, sometimes. The feel of a little peepee in my ass is really nice. If the boy is old enough to come, I come when he does. If he's not old enough to come, I come when I get in his ass.

Yes, I really do stuff like this. I've served time for child-molesting and manslaughter. I killed a kid once. I fucked him in the mouth so hard, he suffocated. What a great way to go. Fucked in the mouth till you die. I'm getting hard just thinking about it. Once I was fucking a kid and his mother caught us. She was a very sorry lady, I can assure you. I chained the kid up and made his mother blow me in front of him. Then I put a bottle up in her ass and made her blow her own kid. She threw up, and I loved it. I unchained him and made him fuck her in both the cunt and the ass. Afterwards, I kicked the shit out of both of them as an incentive not to tell the husband, a cop. They told, and I got put away.

I hang around schoolyards in white neighborhoods. I pick up kids this way. After I get to know them, I take them to drugstores and buy them things. I come on real friendly. When I get them to where I live, I tell them I have done terrible things in my life and I'm sorry. I tell them it would make me happy if they would punish me. They handcuff my hands to the bedposts and manacle my feet and beat me with the whips I have. I'm on my back so I can watch them work me over. When my cock gets hard, sometimes one of the kids will get all excited and blow me. If nobody blows me, I come by myself anyhow. When the kids are through with me, they turn me loose and leave. I always have one kid stay behind. I chain him up and use the whip on him and fuck him in the ass. After this, I turn the kid loose and leave. I'm an ironworker and can find work anywhere in the country. I've lived in a lot of towns, I'll tell you.

I stick pins in myself and cut myself with razors or nails or whatever I can get my hands on. My ears and nose are pierced. I drove a nail through the palm of my hand once. Nailed myself to a board and then jerked off to the pain. I came automatically when I yanked the nail out.

I had an aunt who used to let me fuck her when I was a kid. She was my first piece of ass. When she'd finish with me, she'd grab my cock and balls and twist them till I howled and tell me what a nasty little fucker I was to fuck my own aunt. Then, the next day, she'd be back fucking me again. She used to jam Coke bottles in her cunt and make me fuck her in the ass while she did it. Then she'd suck the shit off my dick and make me fuck her. Then she'd slap me around and tell me how nasty I was and how she was going to tell my mother on me. I knew she'd never do that. My mother supported us. The aunt was my babysitter.

I was the one who told my mother. From then on, on weekends, my mother used to watch my aunt and me go at it while she worked on herself with a Coke bottle. When my aunt was through, they'd both punish me. Every now and again, my mother would bring one of the neighbors over to watch. Sometimes, whoever came over would get all excited watching my aunt and me and would wind up doing stuff to my mother. But the end was always the same. I'd get punished and called nasty.

I put a pencil up my cock once. It really hurt good. I wish it was possible. I'd like some guy to shove an umbrella up my ass and open it and pull it out. I've had umbrellas up my ass, but only their handles. I put the rods from work up there sometimes. They're rough and cold and really feel fine.

I have a bicycle chain here that's covered with a plastic tube to keep it from chipping the paint on the bike. I grease it and stuff it up my ass. When I get it all in except for about eight inches or so, I start jerking off. Just as I am going to come, I yank the whole thing out and really have a great orgasm. I fainted once doing this it felt (so good).

* * * *

The last two words in the last paragraph are parenthetical to indicate that I didn't actually hear them. I assume he ended the sentence with words to that effect. I hung up and quit writing the book for about a month and did two fast magazine articles that were not related to sex. I can't tell you how nice it was not even to think about whips and chains and screams of pain from children. Even with the passage of time, it is difficult to read this man's fantasy unemotionally. Such fantasies, and particularly the behavior they represent, remain incomprehensible to me. And frightening.

AFTERWORD

The book is done. Often I enjoyed the work that went into it. At other times I hated the information I was gathering. I was never bored.

A psychiatrist friend has carefully read the manuscript. He says the book will be useful and will ease the fears and guilts many have about the content of their erotic imaginings. If the book is helpful, I should be content. Yet I am not. The research that went into the book revealed to me something I had not known; there is more sadness than I had supposed. There is humor and joy in some of the book's material, but it is engulfed and overwhelmed by the sadness and the loneliness.

Think about what it must be like to be that aging dishwasher who likes to spank young men and have "annual" sex with them. He has no education; he's getting old; he lives in his fantasies and books and movies; he's having trouble finding partners; his wife has left him; and with the passage of the years, he can expect increasing solitude and contempt to be his lot. One day he will be too old to wash dishes and too feeble to seek out the kind of love he needs. What a terrible and degrading destiny. I have that man's name and address and telephone number. I could call him on the telephone now and again, I suppose, and offer him words of encouragement and cheer. But I won't do it. He repels me, and I don't want to talk to him, or even think about him, ever again. There is a callousness in me that I had not known was there.

Think about that delivery boy who claims to rape women in Queens, New York. Do happy men call strangers on the telephone to groan and giggle and masturbate while confessing felonies and thinking about real or imagined visitations of pain upon their neighbors? Does a man like that have any friends? I doubt it. I imagine he drives his delivery bike around the cold and indifferent city dreaming his terrible dreams alone and friendless and unnoticed. And when he is noticed and people shy back when they see the flicker of madness glittering behind his eyes, does this cause him pain? Will he kill some hapless woman or child someday in revenge for whatever hellish childhood he had? I feel sorry for this man. But I also fear him. Will he one day deliver groceries to my wife or someone else I know and love? Or someone you know and love?

"I am a married fag with children. I think I will kill myself." This man's voice was strangled with emotion. In the second before he returned the telephone to its cradle, I heard a sob. Can you imagine the weight of sadness this man must carry with him through all his days and nights? And the unending fear of discovery that gnaws at him?

"They're all whores, every goddamn one of them . . ." This man expresses contempt for half the human race. In what way was he wounded to produce a reaction so stifling and destructive? Who will he hurt under the urgings of his delusion?

I cannot count the number of late-night telephone calls I received from men offering to fellate me. All perfect strangers, most earnest and polite. How alone they must be to call strangers, and how sharp must be the sting of rejection.

I think the most disturbing aspect to the materials gathered here is the general lovelessness of most of it. Sex, I was raised to believe, has something to do with warmth and affection and tenderness and the other attributes of love. But most of the sex in this book has to do with sex alone. Most of the people who told me their fantasies are telling me about ways they have had orgasms, or wish they had had orgasms. When the word *love* comes into the interviews, it is usually in the context of "I love it" and not in the setting of "I love her" or "I love him." A pall of inhumanity hangs over much of what is reported. I find it disquieting. I have known for a long time that love is rare. I had not known that it is virtually nonexistent.

Equally disturbing is the quantity of violence in the materials herein. Nancy Friday has written a book called *My Secret Garden*. Like this book, it is a collection of sexual fantasies. Female sexual fantasies. For the most part, the fantasies she gathered in her years of work are gentler than those reported to me. Some of the fantasies in her book are dark and cruel. But very few. Is there a conclusion to be drawn from this? Was there some flaw in the way I gathered my materials? I strove for an entirely random sampling. The interviews were conducted with men from every walk of life; the only commonality among them was their willingness to supply material for the book. Perhaps men who are willing to discuss their fantasies are crueler than other men. I hope so. If the world were peopled with as many monsters as I have uncovered, it would be an even more frightening place than it already is.

I thought years ago when I began gathering materials for the book that I would end up with a collection of dreams and wishes that would give us a mirror in which we could see ourselves clearer than in the past. I hope, most sincerely, that this is not a mirror but some freakishly distorted glass that has an uncanny ability to filter out joy and beauty while magnifying sadness and ugliness. But, although I hope this, I fear I hope in vain.

Matthew Arnold noted in the last century that the world has neither joy, nor love, nor light, nor certitude, nor peace, nor help for pain. I have always thought that Arnold vastly overstated the case for gloom. I still think so. But not vastly.